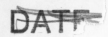

SO-ARX-770

Skid Row, U.S.A.

Books by Sara Harris

SKID ROW, U.S.A.
FATHER DIVINE: HOLY HUSBAND
THE WAYWARD ONES

Skid Row, U.S.A.

BY SARA HARRIS

1956

DOUBLEDAY & COMPANY, INC.

GARDEN CITY, NEW YORK

Library of Congress Catalog Card Number 55–8401

Copyright © 1956 by Sara Drucker Harris
All Rights Reserved
Printed in the United States of America at
The Country Life Press, Garden City, N.Y.
Designed by Alma Reese Cardi
First Edition

TO MY FATHER

Contents

Foreword

This book is perhaps the first clear portrayal of the group of lost souls that constitute Skid Row. It is a commentary on society's callous indifference that most of us are hardly aware that such persons exist. This is true despite the fact that every city throughout the country has its Skid Row reeking with tragedy and sadness, souls born in the image of God living in a valley of fear and apprehension. Seldom do they smile. Seldom do they feel affection for anyone. Theirs is an empty life.

The beauty of this book is that it offers us an opportunity to understand these people, to understand how they became what they are, and to determine how we might make it otherwise. Essentially, these are undersocialized men and women, human beings whose early life lacked the nourishment of normal affection, normal human understanding; human beings who as they passed into adolescence did not have the opportunity to develop healthy relationships with other youngsters, human beings who as they passed into maturity developed a fear, an insecurity that either made impossible or rendered difficult the establishment of a marital relationship. In this uncertainty they frequently seek an escape in demon rum. They are either true alcoholics or at the least their life is colored by excessive drinking.

Society's answer today is the flophouse or the prison cell, either of which is calculated to make more certain the further degradation of these unfortunates. By reading the profound interpretations of the lives presented in these pages it is to be hoped that we, the more fortunate, will be shocked into a deeper understanding. It is to be hoped, too, that society will attempt to provide more than a flop or a cell. With God's grace, any or all of these lost souls could regain self-respect and assume a relatively normal place in society.

John M. Murtagh
Chief Magistrate of the City of New York

Skid Row, U.S.A.

1. "All Kinds Types"

Madmen, feeble-minded folk, cripples, and blind people live along Skid Row, U.S.A. So do prostitutes, called "fleabags," because they are inclined to be syphilitic, and a few old egocentric fighters against society. Respectable old people live along Skid Row on pensions and old-age insurances. And young, able-bodied men live there, because they have lost all semblance of faith in God, humanity, or themselves.

Skid Rowers comprise well over fifty per cent of the county jail population of every city in this country. Many, but not all of them, are addictive drinkers. They sometimes get alcoholic convulsions or delirium tremens so that they must be restrained in insane asylums or psychopathic wards of general hospitals. Some of them die of starvation or exposure to freezing weather and are buried in potter's fields. Experts estimate that, between jailing them for vagrancy or intoxication and hospitalizing and burying them, we are spending well over forty-five million dollars a year on their keep.

Skid Row, U.S.A., belches despair. Skid Rowers consider it "the last step before the grave." They wash their hands of themselves and say they're beyond caring what happens to them any more. Nobody else cares either. We have always been casual about Skid Row and have secured no adequate facts about its inhabitants. We do not even know exactly how many people live or die or have accidents along Skid Row, U.S.A.

When I first started to look into Skid Row, U.S.A., I sought the co-operation of the agencies that worked with Rowers—hospital emergency wards, courts, city welfare departments, missions. This book could not have been written had it not been for the help I received from the staffs of all these organizations. But there are many Rowers who do not come within the ken of any rehabilitative agency. So I also cultivated flophouse managers and proprietors of the restaurants known as "greasy spoons" along the Row and owners of the low-down bars called "bloody buckets." I met many more of the people I have recorded in this book in saloons than in social agencies.

It is hard to make contact in Skid Row saloons. Most people who hang out in them drink for oblivion, not a lift. You're lucky when you find them awake and able to talk to you. Besides, most Rowers no longer remember what your world is all about, and you're bound to be a foreigner in theirs.

I took a long time learning how to approach Skid

Rowers and how to evaluate the different ways they approached me. One thing I am glad about in retrospect, I was always honest. I never attempted to pose as a Skid Rower. I told everyone I talked to that I was on the Row to write a book. Some of them were resentful and told me to mind my own business. Some said a book would be "very nice." Many, who had been on Skid Row so long that they'd lost all touch with everyone who was not of themselves except for missionaries, tried to take what they considered advantage of me in the same way they take advantage of the men and women who are there to salvage their souls for Christ. I could almost gauge what they were thinking while they talked to me—well, sure, give her a good story, the harder luck the better. Go on, tell her what you told that Hallelujah Boy at Sunshine Gospel Mission last Sunday, tell her how life started beating the stuffing out of you before you was born, go on, tell her, she'll believe you, the Hallelujah Boy did. In a sense these men "sang for their supper" with me as they were accustomed to doing with missionaries. They told me their so-called stories and then sat around waiting for me to buy them glasses of wine or plates of bacon and eggs.

Most Skid Rowers are not like that though. They neither resent you as an outsider nor approve you nor compose life stories for you. They haven't the energy. They just are, and when they stop being, they die. As simply as that. Talking to them, trying to probe inside them, gets you no place. Not because they want to stop you from probing. On the contrary. Some of them would like to help you know them. Really, they want very much to help you find out why they are what they have become—in some long-forgotten part of them they are interested to know themselves—but they can't help you, because their minds and hearts are too much blunted today. So they sit with you around the scarred wooden tables of the Gold Pheasant Bar in Philadelphia or the Sunshine in Chicago, and they listen to you while you talk to them about how "there is a way out for you, man," and they nod their heads, but all the time they don't believe you. They let you think they do but inside they don't, because they have a philosophy of hopelessness built up over years of living on the Row.

Of course everyone on the Row feels hopeless. They wouldn't be here if they didn't. But the ones I am talking about are the most hopeless of all. That is the only reason they are here, when you come right down to it. That is their only handicap. They are not like those other people you see on the Row, that young girl, for example, with the mad green eyes and the tangled brown hair who spat full in the face of a Bowery officer and told him, "Listen, cop, I'll go with niggers so long's white ones looks like you." Knowing all the time she'd be pulled in. Or should have known if she'd been mentally well. Or like Gerald O'Mahoney who hangs out along Sand Street in Brooklyn and spends most of his days crying over the plight of the residents of New Rochelle. "They starve to death," he maintains. Hostile voices tell him he is responsible too. "O'Mahoney," they say, "New Rochelle is all your fault." These people I am talking about are not like the blind people called "blinkies" to their faces around here or the crippled ones called "crips." They have their eyes and legs and the ability to maintain reality with their environment. That is, they know where they are. Only thing, they've lost the faculty for caring much.

Skid Row, U.S.A., can't come clear to people in a day or a month. Its desperate sameness is too confusing. For example, you can't begin to distinguish the differences between Skid Row, New York, and Skid Row, San Francisco, at first. The physical likenesses are too keen. The street names and sizes vary. That's all. Vermin-ridden, firetrap flophouses charging fifty cents for lying down in a single bed with a clean sheet and two blankets and fifteen cents for a flop on a dormitory floor. Greasy spoon restaurants with fancy names selling hash and onions or spaghetti and meatballs for twenty cents and featuring delicacies like bacon and eggs or pigs' snouts for forty-five. Missions offering free beds and meals in the name of Jesus Christ. And saloons, four or five on every block, running the gamut all the way from respectable enough to accommodate tourists by night to bloody buckets where anything can happen.

Sit in bloody buckets long enough and you'll meet all the Rowers there. The ones with money come to drink and the ones without to mooch. Besides, bloody buckets are the nearest approaches to social clubs that Skid Row, U.S.A., happens to have. Even the few Rowers who are not heavy drinkers come to bloody buckets to meet their friends.

I first met the man who helped me a great deal with the writing of this book in a bloody bucket. I never found out his real name. His nickname is Schloime the Troime. That is a Jewish nickname meaning Sam the Dreamer. And if ever a man fitted his nickname, Schloime the Troime is that one. He is tall and skinny with dangling arms and hands that can't be still. He has a long nose and a small mouth with protruding teeth. His eyes are brown and soft. His hair is white and always looks as though he has just had it cut around a bowl. In the winter, Schloime wears dark green corduroy pants and a red-and-black checked lumberjacket buttoned over a badly torn undershirt. In the summer, on any day that the temperature exceeds eighty-three, he dispenses with the lumberjacket. On these days he always carries it over his right arm.

One time, on a particularly hot summer day, I spoke to him about that lumberjacket. "It's so hot," I said, "why not leave the lumberjacket in your room?"

Schloime regarded me for a long, uncomfortable moment. He said, "By me, it's like the lady gets a new mink coat. In her life, summer makes some difference? Ha?"

It wasn't till a long time later, after I knew it on my own and Schloime had begun to trust me, that he explained that his lumberjacket would doubtless be stolen if he were to leave it in any one of the flops he went to.

"Tch, tch, tch," he said when he told me. "Poor little people got to steal to live. It's very sorrowful, yes?"

Schloime the Troime came to the Bowery thirty-seven years ago. Before that, he'd used to work "someplace in some shop." He doesn't care to talk much about those pre-Skid Row years, but he is too polite to resist if you press him. "Well, in that shop, it was very bad. No time to do nothing, only work, work. Say like a poem comes in mine head, working in that shop, I can't stop to write. The big boss says no. By him is his money more important than mine brain." He stops, overcome himself by this supreme example of human selfishness. "Imagine it? If I didn't get this idea I should walk right out from that job, it could be now I'd be broke on the wheel of labor. No time I should look up to the stars. Now, I can look up all I want. Maybe mine clothes is lousy, but don't feel sorry. Whenever I want, I stop and look up to the stars."

But Schloime the Troime, an individualist in his way, albeit a ragged one, and a man who is secure in the fact that, no matter how sordid his environment, he has chosen it himself, is a fair rarity in these parts. And nobody knows that better than Schloime.

"You shouldn't make a big mistake and judge here by me," he says. "Most men ain't here for looking up to stars. They don't even know, poor little people, is stars or is not. Many of them is not here because they want but only because what else is?"

That was the knowledge of Schloime. I was lucky to have met him, and I know that he guided me into alleys and byways I never could have entered without him. And he did more than that. He taught me a code of behavior for this strange new world that I doubtless never could have evolved for myself. Often his teaching was subtle, but sometimes, as on the day when I met a Bowery lady named Pig Head Hattie, it was about as direct as any teaching I have ever experienced.

I met Pig Head in an alley off the Bowery. Schloime introduced us with all the graciousness of a potentate bringing a couple of favored subjects together. I took my cue from him.

"Mrs. Harris," he said, "I am happy you should make the acquaintance with Miss Pig Head Hattie."

I said, "How do you do, Miss Hattie?"

Pig Head Hattie looked at me, obviously trying to see beneath my formality and to weigh it for what it might be worth.

"What you calling me Miss for?" she asked. "The whole name's Pig Head Hattie but everybody calls me Pig Head. If Pig Head is too long to say, you can call me Pig for short." And added, "If you keep on seeing me around and want to call me anything at all."

I ignored the speculation and said, "Pig Head is not too long to say."

How to describe Pig Head Hattie? I suppose you would have to begin with her legs. They are thick and shapeless, seeming not to belong with the rest of her long, skinny body. On the day I met her, she wore two different stockings, a flesh-colored nylon on the right one and a black lisle on the left. The flesh nylon was run so profusely and so neatly that the runs, at first look, seemed to be a planned-out and highly intricate new stocking design.

She has blue eyes that water. Her sight is bad, but she has never worn glasses. Once, when she could not help herself and had to go to New York's municipal lodging house for a flop, a lady social worker who interviewed her suggested she see an eye doctor at the city's expense. Pig Head would like to have seen an eye doctor.

"I said to that social worker, I said, 'Thanks, lady, thanks a lot. Anything the city's going to do for me will be appreciated by yours truly and also by her father and mother looking down from above.'"

The municipal social worker never followed up on getting Pig Head to the doctor. Pig Head doesn't know whether she forgot about her suggestion or got involved in other things.

"I wouldn't hold nobody to blame if she went and forgot," Pig Head said. "All that poor girl had to do. It's a big, holy wonder to me she used to remember what was her name."

I asked Pig Head why, since she knew that the social worker was busy and likely to forget about her, she hadn't reminded her about the doctor.

Pig Head looked as though I had stuck knives into her. "God!" she said disgustedly.

Apologetically, without knowing why I felt that way, I said, "If I've said anything to hurt your feelings——"

"God!" Pig Head said. "If you said *anything! If* you said anything. If you *said* anything. *God!*"

I said, "I'm sorry, Pig. Whatever it is for."

"Well, you should be," she said. "Do you think just because it happened to so happen you met me on the Bowery, a girl ain't got her pride? Me remind one of them lousy, crawling social workers anything? I got my pride same's the next one or you, yourself, too. I got my pride. Jesus Christ, Mary and Joseph, yessirree God. I know what's eating you. You heard some of them lousy bottle bums call me a fleabag. You think I go with them for a quarter, thirty cents. Well, you're barking up the wrong tree, sister, see? The least I ever went with one of them bums for was half a buck. Plenty of times they paid me dollars. This girl's got her pride. Anyone don't think so can drop dead. You too, sister."

I didn't know how to answer Pig. I looked at Schloime the Troime for help in interpreting myself to her. "Please, Schloime," I said, "tell her I didn't mean to hurt her feelings. Try to make her understand. I know she has her pride and up until today I hadn't heard anything about her—business. I would never have suggested she check up on that social worker if I had thought anything of it. I mean, if I had been in Pig's place, I would have checked on the social worker. It seems to me that 'pride' hasn't got so much to do with it."

"It seems to you!" Pig Head said sarcastically.

On that day Schloime the Troime gave me the most open lesson I have ever had from him. He placed a skinny hand on my shoulder. "You know," he said, "by Miss Hattie is the right more than by you. Here, in her world, is pride one thing. There, where you live is pride another thing. Now the way it happens, you are where she lives. When you come in where you don't live, it means you don't know how is things. So, what is for you to do? Find out. And the mouth, you should keep it closed."

"Yeah, closed!" Pig Head said.

I said, "I'm sorry, Schloime! And Pig!"

Schloime said, "It's nothing to be so sorry. When you become old like me is the keeping quiet will come more natural."

Pig said, "Yeah, but she ought to know it now. So damn young she ain't." And that, more right than wrong on her part, as Schloime the Troime would say, was the next to the last hostile remark Pig Head Hattie ever made to me.

The last one, some few weeks after I'd met her and was buying her and Schloime lunch in a clean cafeteria on Delancey Street off the Bowery was this: "You walk around here trying to bring your nose down out of the air. You think you got us fooled. Go on, you ain't fooling nobody. Everybody's got your number. All you're doing around here is you're looking for types. I met a lady writer one time, she came from a newspaper though, said that right out."

That time Schloime the Troime defended me vigorously. "So, Pig Head Hattie, are you a very smart woman. You got it all figured out that's what she does. Nu, so when did she ever say no? She didn't tell you right away, 'I'm writing a book?' So, sure she's looking for types. That's bad, maybe? Believe me, it's very, very good. She should only tell the true what it is she finds here." He turned to me. "You should only tell the honest and true is all I want. Come on. I know where is plenty types, all kinds types down here."

Schloime the Troime is right about "all kinds types"

down here, but you've got to know Skid Row before you can begin to realize that.

Skid Row, U.S.A., to anyone who does not really know it from inside, is that place where alcoholics on their last legs have come to drink in peace. You see them every day all right, the same on Sunday as on Monday, no holidays here, guzzling in the bloody buckets where they can rest their aching heads or else drinking outside the saloons, handmade sneaky pete or bay rum or hair tonic or cheap perfume snitched from the five and dime, or you see them passed out, lying on sidewalks or sprawled out in gutters.

There are "all kinds types" among the crazy, blind-drunk ones too, however. Skid Row, U.S.A., is not, as the stereotype would have it, primarily a refuge for addictive alcoholics from other and far higher places. It is that, of course, but incidentally, not primarily. If you want to find alcoholic doctors, lawyers, sons of millionaires, and college professors you will doubtless find some here. This is where they live. But they do not comprise a majority. One fact I learned early in my contact along Skid Row, U.S.A., was this. Many more people drink because they are here than are here because they drink.

Why did they hit the Row in the first place then? That is a question that cannot be answered by generalizing. "All kinds types" necessarily means "all kinds reasons." And if this work clarifies that fact, it will have served its purpose.

2. Apples of Their Mothers' Eyes

The most irredeemable Skid Rowers are, paradoxically, the young and able-bodied men. There are many of them. As a matter of fact, they outnumber all the other Rowers put together. They don't believe in God and they hate people. Some of them hate all people, and some hate all people except their mothers whom they adore. But most of their mothers are dead by the time they have reached Skid Row.

Most able-bodied Rowers are contemptuous of themselves. They believe they are on Skid Row because they deserve to be. They are dyed-in-the-wool fatalists. They aren't angry over their situations and they don't whine about them. They merely go on existing day after hopeless day with the feeling that what's bound to happen to them will happen.

Thirty-three-year-old Billy Brams is like that. He doesn't look as if he would be, what with his strong, bull body, but he is, all the same. I met him first on Chicago's main stem and later in New York. We didn't talk very much in Chicago, but we got friendly in New York. We often met casually at Collins's on the Bowery. One day I asked Billy whether there was someplace I could contact him if I ever wanted to talk to him by appointment. He spread his beefy hands out so that they almost covered Collins's table for two and talked to me while he made animated finger motions and watched them.

"Yeah," he said, "sure, Logan's flop. I got six bucks. Guess I'll stay around Logan's till I run out of it."

I said, "Where'll you go when you do run out?"

He said, "Aah."

I said, "Look, Billy, you know what month this is?"

He said, "Yeah, sure, November, so?"

I said, "So November's not a warm month."

Billy grinned. "So who don't know that?"

I said, "Look, Billy, I've known some freezing Novembers in New York. Suppose this turns out to be a cold one too and if you don't stay at Logan's and you've got no money for another flop and you won't go to the 'Hallelujah Boys,' what will you do?"

Billy shrugged his shoulders.

I said, "You can't just sleep outdoors in winter."

"Maybe I won't need to," he said.

I said, "But maybe you will. Right?"

He nodded.

"Doesn't it worry you, Billy?"

"Worry?" he asked, as though the word had never been

in his vocabulary. "Worry? What good would worrying do?"

"But, Billy," I said, "for heaven's sake, don't you believe that you have anything to do with the things that happen to you? For instance, don't you believe that you can do something to prevent your having to sleep outdoors in winter?"

"Me?" Billy almost choked with the laughter he tried to suppress because he figured he might hurt my feelings if he didn't. "Me?"

I said, "Don't you think you have anything at all to do with the way you live?"

Now Billy couldn't control his laughter any more. It came spurting out of him. And that was my answer. So I began probing him about whys and wherefores. I tried to find out exactly when this feeling that he held no responsibility for his own life had begun in him. He tried to tell me but he couldn't.

He kept shaking his head over and over again. "Look, I don't know, I just don't know, that's all." Still he kept on trying with me and answered my specific questions as well as he was able. "My old man? Yeah, he was O.K. I guess. What's there to tell about him? Just a guy like everybody else. What do you mean loved him? He was my old man, wasn't he? My ma? She was O.K. too. Yeah. What do you mean done for me? Hell, yeah, she used to tell me what was right and wrong. When there was eats in the house, she always give me some. She was good like that. Yeah, I got three brothers. No, no sisters. My broth-

ers, yeah, they was O.K. too, I guess. What are they doing now? How the hell'd I know what they was doing
now? Excuse my expression. Still alive? Yeah, I guess. I
don't really know if they're still alive. Yeah, sure, we lost
touch. What we got to keep in touch for? Them do something for me? Well, jeez, I don't expect nothing like that."

I went on questioning Billy Brams, trying to find out
when he first lost his faith in people. I asked him whether
he remembered ever having expected anyone to do anything for him, and he said no.

"I always knew nobody'd do nothing for nothing," he
said. "When I was just a little kid I found out if people
done something for you, they expected you should do twice
as much for them."

I said, "People sometimes do things for other people
because they like them, Billy."

He laughed.

I said, "Say, Billy, you had girl friends, didn't you?"

"A couple."

I asked if he'd ever thought his girl friends liked him,
and he said he'd never thought anything about whether
they did or not.

"Did they say they liked you?" I asked.

"Yeah, sure, they said it. What do you expect, they
wouldn't say it? Course I never believed any of them."

"Why would they say they liked you if they didn't,
Billy?"

"How'd I know? I'm no mind reader." Then after having

thought for a while he added, "I used to keep jobs in those days."

"Are you sure it was your jobs?" I asked.

He said, "Couldn't be nothing else."

I said, "Did you ever look in the mirror, Billy? You're not a bad-looking man, you know."

He burst out laughing. "What are you telling me things like that? I'm a slob."

I said, "Sure, your clothes are dirty and I can't tell from the looks of your face when you last had a razor near it. But you'd be surprised at what a good-looking fellow you'd turn out to be if you did shave and get into some clean clothes."

He laughed again but he was flattered. "You excuse me for saying so, you must need glasses."

I said, "I've got an idea. Get cleaned up and see for yourself."

At first he said he thought he would but I told him I didn't think so and then he admitted that he didn't think he would either and we talked for hours about why he wouldn't. Only two ideas came out of our talk. He was really nobody so why should he pretend to be somebody and even if he did pretend, who was going to believe him anyway?

The same questions I'd heard from numerous Skid Rowers ever since I'd first begun reporting them. Who cares about me? What do I matter in the world? And the same unvarying answers based on the fact that these men are what their environment has somehow made of them, suspicious, rootless folk with no faith in God or in people and above all with no feeling of self-dignity. That is why they go through their miserable days with the idea that they have no control whatever over their own lives.

You've got to spend a long time along Skid Row before you can begin to know how truly egoless these men are, and you can't begin to appreciate the extent of their dependence on fate until you know that. And when you do find it out you will know that you have never understood the depths of human misery until now. For here are hundreds of thousands of people who live in degradation and who accept it because they feel they deserve no better and because they haven't enough energy to conceive being anyplace else.

"Where else would I go if I came off here?" red-haired, pug-nosed Jimmy Ferguson asked me over lunch.

I said, "This is a big country."

He said, "For you maybe."

I said, "For you too."

He said, "Hell."

I said, "Did you ever stop to think what can happen to you if you don't leave here?"

"Sure," he said. "I'll die in jail."

I said, "Not necessarily."

"All right," he said, "so it'll be the booby hatch. I got a couple of friends in Bellevue nut house now. Holy Jesus Christ. I went there to visit my friends one time and I never went back. One of my friends weighed seventy-six pounds after he'd been in that psycho ward awhile. Seventy-six pounds! And he used to be kind of a fat guy too. Can you imagine it? He stayed fat all the time he lived on the Bowery although he was always hungry as a bear. Then they took him to the hospital was supposed to be making him feel better and he got so skinny. Another friend of mine was in Psycho too. He's out now. He says it's terrible there. He'd rather die than go back." He stopped talking for a while and rested his head in his hands. Then he looked up at me. "I know more'n you think," he said, "a man might as well be dead as down here."

I said, "You've got to get out if you know that."

He said, "How could I anyways?"

I said, "There are people who'll help you if you'll only let them."

"Who?" he asked. "The Hallelujah Boys? I hate their guts."

I said, "The missionaries aren't the only ones who want to help you."

He said, "Oh, no?" And he added, "What can they do anyways? I mean even if they wanted to, there's nothing. There's nothing anybody can do. I mean just nothing."

I first met Jimmy Ferguson at the Bowery Mission in New York. I saw him sitting in the fourth pew of the small chapel that, without its hosts of strange-looking worshipers, would have the feel and look of any other small chapel, under a sign that read: "Come, All Ye That Are Heavy Laden and Lay Your Burdens Down." I sat beside him. A strong stench emanated from him. I had to brace myself to stand it. I smiled at him. He didn't smile back.

"I'm no nose diver, lady," he whispered, "like some of these other characters. I only come in here to get warm, that's all."

He had sensitive hands with long fingernails that contained long-lodged dirt. He kept sucking inside his nails. I judged him to be about thirty-one or thirty-two, maybe a year or so younger.

Jimmy wouldn't have known it, of course, but I had seen him once before, some six weeks earlier on Third Street, a few blocks off the Bowery. Now, he wore an old navy-blue shirt, with long sleeves that flapped, but then he hadn't worn any shirt or coat at all. In daylight and full view of passers-by, he had tapped the engine of a 1952 De Soto and lain on the cold street, naked from the chest up, holding his mouth open to catch the alcohol as it spouted out of the engine. I'll never forget the dead-pan look of his face as he sucked the alcohol. Now he sat half asleep and half listening to the man who stood on the platform and told how he had been the "lowest of the low," raggedy pants, no shirt, no food to eat, every dime he could beg or steal going to keep him in liquor. In his own mind he had been a doomed man, he said. He'd been murdering himself. Many kind people had tried to help him. He had been entirely beyond anybody's help and had known it. Then, Christ came to him. The coming might seem sudden to some but not to him as he reflected upon it now. For God had caused him to touch bottom so that there would be no ounce of pride left to keep him from opening up his heart. He said, "I was sitting right here in this very mission when I heard the words that saved me. 'Jesus died for you.' Oh, that really struck me; it was something I never knew before that Jesus died for me. Oh, it was so beautiful. I never knew before anybody loved me enough to die for me."

I looked at Jimmy. A part of him seemed impressed by the testimony he was hearing. "Maybe he's a nose diver," he said, less to me than to himself. "Maybe not. Aw, sure, he is. Everybody in these joints nose dives."

When the service was over, the men were invited to come downstairs for coffee and peanut butter and jelly sandwiches. They waited in line to get their food and ate it standing up. I stood beside Jimmy while he ate his.

He said, "I didn't put anything over on nobody. I told the guy runs this mission that I'm cold and hungry but I'm not going on my knees. God never done nothing for me, so why should I go on my knees for Him? I was surprised when that mission guy told me I could stay and eat anyways. I don't know why he did it or what he thinks he can get out of me."

I told him that I knew Mr. Anderson, the assistant superintendent to whom he had reference, to be a former Skid Rower himself. I said, "Of course, he aims to convert you to Jesus in the long run. But if he can't do that, he wants to help you now, anyhow. Believe me, he doesn't want to get anything out of you."

"Yeah, yeah," Jimmy said.

Jimmy Ferguson was born on a farm in Kansas. He tells

about his childhood and family relationships with unique objectivity.

"Our farm was a stinker for growing things. My old man used to work hard, I'll give him that credit anyways, but it didn't do any good. There was five other kids besides me. The old man used to smack us all with a horsewhip. My back side was always sore. My ma was a-scared of him. She got a heart attack and dropped dead when I was thirteen."

Jimmy got into trouble with the law when he was fourteen. He and an older brother stole seven dollars from a neighboring farmer.

"The guy said he was going to get me and my brother put in jail. I asked my old man was it true. He said, sure it was true. I asked my old man was he going to do anything to try changing the guy's mind. Well, he didn't need to tell me no. I knew he wasn't going to. He'd rather have me in jail than home eating up his produce. So I ran away one night."

He began walking toward Kansas City. He supported himself by "house-catting," begging food at people's back doors. Since he was young and small for his age, housewives always fed him well. He slept in barns when he could find them, in forests and open fields when he couldn't.

I said, "People were kind to you on the road, weren't they?"

Jimmy said, "Kind? The farm women gave me food if that's what you mean, but they made me sing for my supper. They enjoyed crying over me." He lifted his voice in mocking imitation, " 'Oh you poor little thing.' No, they didn't give me food just because they were good people. Don't kid yourself."

After he'd been tramping the road for several weeks, Jimmy ran into an older, experienced tramp named Red Bill. Red Bill was a big, brawny man with red hair and a deep voice. As Jimmy was to discover over a period of years he was to spend with him, Red Bill was the kind of man who took what he wanted whenever he wanted it and no questions asked. He wanted Jimmy as soon as he saw him.

Jimmy said, "At first I didn't know what he wanted out of me. He said, 'Let's you and me be a team, kid.' I said, 'If we was to be a team, won't I be too much trouble to you?' He said, 'A cute little fellow like you trouble? You and me's going to have some fun.' I was a dumb kid who didn't know anything about 'jockers' and 'punks.' So, when he said he'd be my jocker and I'd be his little punk and that meant he was going to show me the ropes on the road, I said O.K. Then when nighttime came, I found out what it meant to be a punk. I didn't like it. We were sleeping in this barn and I told him, jeez, no, Bill. He didn't like a jerk like I was saying no to him. He said, 'Listen, kid, I'm the kind of jocker never begs my punks. I tell them! Then he kind of swing his fist out and knocked me down."

After the first night he spent with him, Jimmy recognized himself as Bill's official punk. There were times at the beginning of the relationship when he thought he might run away from Red Bill. He never attempted to. Firstly, because Bill threatened him. He said that if Jimmy ever tried to run away he would be sure to find him, and that when he did he'd kick him in the head until his whole face was bloody and he passed out cold. Secondly and more importantly, he did not attempt to run away because his pattern of relying on fate to mold his life was clearly established by the time he met Red Bill. Besides the self-contempt was already strong in him.

"Anyways," he says, "who was I to say no when Red Bill said yes?"

Red Bill and Jimmy headed for New York where they flopped together. They supported themselves by begging on the streets. Jimmy became a successful panhandler due to his youthful appearance. Red Bill had a more effective technique. He was able to manipulate his body in such a way that he could appear to be a paralytic. Today, Jimmy tells how "Red Bill was the best stiffy in New York. I got to hand it to him for that."

Red Bill liked sneaky pete, and he and his pals got Jimmy drinking it. By the time he was sixteen, Jimmy Ferguson was guzzling sneaky. "Listen," he tells today, "everybody else was drinking. That's life on the Row. At first I used to worry because I didn't like the taste of it. Wasn't that too bad about me? *I* didn't like the goddamn taste. Guys'd give me drinks and I used to want to say no. Of course I never did it." How could he have dared? Who was he, after all, to say no to anything?

Bill and Jimmy stayed together till Jimmy was twenty-six years old and Red Bill located himself a younger punk.

Red Bill told him about the new punk. "So long, fella," he said.

Jimmy said, "See you in Frisco, boy. Pinch your punk for me." He says he didn't feel one way or another about Red Bill's leaving him.

I tried to find out his true reactions. "After all," I said, "you and Red Bill were together so many years, you must have felt sorry to lose him."

Jimmy shrugged my idea off.

I asked, "Didn't you feel Red Bill owed you something?"

"How come?" Jimmy asked. "How come? Nobody owes me anything. Not Red Bill. Not nobody."

After Red Bill left, Jimmy went right on living on the Bowery, mooching for a living and drinking sneaky pete. Pals came into his life and walked out of it. World War II began and ended and Jimmy was not concerned. He was an anonymous man beyond the ken of his draft board. One thing World War II did mean in his life, panhandling was a cinch while it was going on but became increasingly difficult after it was over.

"My trouble is," he says, "I always done my mooching straight. I wish I had of learned to act like a crip or something. Red Bill would have been glad to learn me how to look like a stiffy. I sure begun to lose my touch, after the war. Plenty of times I had to 'carry the banner' all night because I couldn't mooch a couple of dimes would buy me a flop."

39

Once I asked Jimmy if he'd ever thought of working for a living. He looked surprised as I'd known he would. "Me? Work? Are you kidding? What the hell for?"

Jimmy poses a legitimate question. Why should such a man want to work? Untrained for any but the most menial kind of labor, no roots anyplace, no attachment to any living person, no feeling about God, and no idea that he deserves any better than what he is presently getting out of life, a bottle of sneaky pete, a flop for the night, a meal when the belly begins to cry for one, what reason would such a man have for working?

I talked to so many men like Jimmy Ferguson, incomplete people, all of them, without egos or faith in anything or anyone. I tried to find out when it was they first stopped feeling human. I said, "When you were twenty-one, sixteen, eight, four?" Blank faces. And the faces were not any cover-up for deep emotions either, but were only manifestations of blank hearts and blank minds. When did it start being this way anyhow?

The egolessness started during early childhood for most of them. It stemmed out of many realities. They were inferior children as a group, neither as strong nor as smart as the others around them. Many, but by no means all of them, came from poor families and lived in overcrowded homes. Some of them came, like Jimmy Ferguson, from homes broken by divorce, separation, or death. Many of them never knew what it meant to be loved by their parents. Paradoxically, however, at least as many were loved

40

too much. But always by their mothers and not ever by anyone else.

Skid Row, U.S.A., is full of adoring sons of adoring mothers. You meet them all over the flops and greasies and bloody buckets. They cry into their wine about what a different place this old world was during the good old days when their sweet little mothers were alive and guiding their destinies for them. If only their mothers hadn't died, they tell you. How they used to trust their mothers. They'd never trusted anybody else in all their lives though. Why should they have? No, they hadn't loved anybody but their mothers either. Never in their lives. Naturally. They'd loved their mothers so much they'd never had room for any other loves in those good old days before they'd hit the Row. Besides, nobody else had ever loved them.

"My ma was the only one ever loved me in the world," Joey Collins said, "and I had nobody after she died."

Big, hearty, bluff Joey Collins with a grip that brought tears to my eyes when we were introduced and shook hands outside Chicago's McCoy Hotel, tough-looking Joey was a mama's boy at forty-seven.

"My ma used to think I was a swell fellow," he said. "I never went to work when she was living. I was the youngest in the family and Ma liked me to stay home and help her around the house. She said I was too weak to work. She got paralyzed when I was thirty-two. My big brother Mikey wanted me to go to work. Ma said nix. She told Mikey like this, 'Joey's the one I want staying home and taking care of me.' Mikey didn't like it. He said, 'Look, Mama, one of the girls'll take care of you better than Joey. He's a fellow. He don't know nothing about cooking or nursing or nothing. He'll screw things up around here. Let Mamie or Marie stay home. Joey'll come work up by my job with me.' Ma said, 'I don't want Mamie or Marie. I ain't got so long to live, my children can't let me have what I want, Michael.' Then she started in bawling. Mikey couldn't stand it so he said, 'O.K. Ma, Joey stays home.' I was sure happy with Mama. Just her and me. I didn't want nobody else."

Big Joey Collins has never heard of modern psychiatry. So he can tell his story uninhibitedly. He does not seek to cover up the silver cord. He admits that he contemplated suicide after his mother died. He knew that nobody else could ever take her place.

"What do I want with anybody but Ma?" he asked. "My brother and sisters, what rats they turned out to be. They didn't cry like me after Mama died. All they done was weep crocodile tears. My brother Michael went and married a stranger, some tomato he never introduced Ma to. Right away he got her knocked up. Now he has her in the old house. Him and her sleeps in Ma's own bed. He stinks like everybody else. I wish I could kill him for insulting my ma. I ain't got the guts, I'm just no good."

Big Joey Collins, whose mother loved him too much but is gone from him now, talks like Jimmy Ferguson who never knew his mother's love. Both men blend together in this melting pot of crooked men and share the same terrible philosophy of life. "I'm just no good. People stinks."

These six words sum up the general psychology of able-bodied Skid Row, U.S.A.

I had never been exposed to such hopelessness before I met it here, and so I found myself mouthing platitudes at the Jimmy Fergusons and the Joey Collinses. I presented them with such stereotypes as, "Where there's a will, there's a way, you know." How laughable! What way for men who just do not possess a will? Why don't they though? Don't they know where they are heading? They know all right. They know more about the jails and asylums and paupers' graves than you ever will.

"So who cares?" they ask, looking at you with half-dead eyes.

Why don't they care? How could they not care about themselves? Nobody knows. Nobody even tried to find out until recently when a few research teams began asking some pertinent questions. Who did these Skid Rowers used to be before they became what they are? Why did they change from what they once were to what they are today? Who failed them? What did society do or neglect to do?

In 1948, the city of San Francisco, induced by the appalling knowledge that $1,690,307.70 out of a total Department of Correction budget of $5,634,359 had been spent for the arrest and incarceration of drunken persons, well over half of them Skid Row repeaters with as many as thirty, forty, fifty, and two hundred arrests to their discredit, undertook a pilot project to investigate Skid Row motivations and to treat a limited number of Skid Row alcoholics. Housed in the San Francisco County Jail and servicing Skid Rowers under arrest, the project was staffed by psychiatrist Joseph Laurie and several psychiatric social workers who, through individual psychiatric interviews combined with a series of therapeutic sessions, arrived at some generalizations of personality types inhabiting Skid Row, U.S.A.

"They are passive and dependent," they reported, "chronic leaners, immature, lacking initiative and self-direction. . . . Some of them are psychopathic with marked anti-social behavior."

Dr. Laurie was the first professional to attach significance to the fact that an unusually large number of men in his group were "the youngest in the family and the apples of their mothers' eyes." Which was not to discount all the negatives that went into the making of Skid Rowers: slum environment, undereducation so that Rowers are equipped to do only unskilled or casual jobs, rejection by their fathers, and a million other less obvious reasons. But above and beyond all these was the mother-son relationship. Sixty per cent of the San Francisco pilot population were either only or youngest children, men in their thirties, forties, fifties, and sixties who still exhibited the strongest attachments for their mothers.

Anyone who has had any contact along Skid Row knows at first hand how much more intense the mother-son attachment is down here than at any other place. Big Joey Collins is only one of many men, unemotional and

44

almost untouchable, whom I shook when I mentioned "your mother."

The very word "mother" holds a fantastic sentimentality on Skid Row, U.S.A. Missionaries know its import from a practical point of view, and so most missions have signs in them along the lines of, "When was the last time you wrote to Mother?" And the Salvation Army finds that mature, motherly types are more effective "soul savers" than the younger lassies are.

Some of the worst fights along the Row happen because somebody makes an uncomplimentary remark about a man's mother, and they are often engaged in by comparative pacificists.

"Son of a bitch" is, without a doubt, the most insulting expression any man can use along the Row.

Elmer Jacobsen, a Philadelphia Rower known for the general profanity of his language even in this place where profanity is so much the rule, grows indignant when he discusses the significance of "son of a bitch."

"Well," he shook a filthy fist in my face as we talked in the New Yorker Bar on Vine Street, "it's such a dirty thing to say. It's an insult. A fellow's saying 'son of a bitch' to me, he knows it's an insult when he ain't talking about me no more, he's talking about my sweet mother. I'll bust his head open. That's all."

Here on Skid Row, U.S.A., men have no need for defenses any more, and so they talk frankly about the relationships they have had with their mothers; and their talk is revealing talk, sometimes sensual in its nostalgia, as though they were discussing long-gone but never-to-be-forgotten sweethearts. And they often tell, without any realization of its meaning, about the warm physical relationships they have known with their mothers.

Johnny DeVito, a small, wizened man who has been hanging around the Philadelphia Skid Row bars for better than twenty of his forty-two years, ever since his mother died, told me how he used to lie in bed with his mother on cold nights.

"Since I was a little fellow I laid in bed with my ma," he said. "Most times the apartments we lived in wasn't warm. So, when I was a baby my ma used to keep me warm laying with me. Her arms was around my body and felt so good. Then when I got big and didn't need nobody to keep me warm no more, well, then, my ma wasn't so young herself and needed I should keep her warm."

Johnny DeVito hated his father as much as he loved his mother. "Him?" he asked. "That ratface? He dropped dead last year. I went back to the old neighborhood one time and a guy told me. I was glad because I always wished it on him."

Skid Rowers talk as uninhibitedly as that, and so the pattern you can only glean in other places is nakedly exposed down here. I met many men who hated their fathers. Some because they loved their mothers. With no more reason than that. The way they lived, there was no room in them for more than one love, and since all their love was expended on their mothers they had nothing to offer their fathers.

Some hated their fathers because of the kinds of men they were. You hear a lot along Skid Row, U.S.A., about fathers who were "drunken bums" with no thought for their families. And about fathers who went "whoring around." You hear a lot about mothers who went out and scrubbed floors to keep their homes together. Their sons are naturally grateful.

But they are grateful to their mothers for everything, even the fact that they bore them. Some Skid Rowers discuss their own births with such affection for detail that you might assume they had been observers from the side lines.

Leslie McGee, forty-one, with a pinhead on tremendous shoulders talked about his birth like this:

"Christ, how my ma suffered when I was born. You can tell I was a big kid. I weighed ten pounds, two ounces. Ma was such a little lady. She carried me in the summertime. You should've saw her July and August. Poor little thing was sweaty with heat. I made her stick out. She was real sick. We were poor so she couldn't get fresh country air like she needed. The doctor she saw before I was born told her she was built small inside. He said if she knew what was good for her, she'd have me with instruments." He banged his hand on the rough, wooden table at Collins's, using it like a gavel. "My ma wasn't scared. She told the doctor he better not use instruments in her because he might hurt my head if he did. The doctor said she might die if he didn't use instruments. She still said no. She told him what were mothers for if not to suffer

47

for their babies. She suffered all right. All the blood came out of her when I was born. She got torn up to pieces."

Leslie McGee feels that he owes a tremendous debt to the mother who bore him, and maybe that's where the overwhelming inferiority feeling first began for him. He must have felt inadequate for paying back the debt from youngest childhood on.

"Sure, sure," he said more vigorously than I have ever heard him say anything else. "I was never good enough to touch the skirts my sweet little ma used to wear."

Many Rowers talk like Leslie McGee.

"My ma's an angel. I don't know how she ever could have got a son like me."

"When I think of my mother I want to lay down and die. I'm ashamed. She's so good and I'm so bad. I don't know what's in me."

Here of all places, along Skid Row, U.S.A., observers must be struck by the frightening fact that mothers with all the good they want for their sons can still do them so much harm sometimes. Don't try telling that to the men though—they'd probably die laughing at you anyhow. Their mothers? *Their* mothers responsible in any way for what has happened to them? Lady, lady, you ought to have your head examined, you're talking loony. You want to blame somebody, all right, blame their old men then.

Most Skid Rowers who love their mothers call their fathers tyrannical. They describe their fathers as they were, ineffectual rather than tyrannical, men who worked at menial jobs and couldn't earn much money. Skid Rowers' mothers seldom respected their fathers.

"My ma always used to wonder what she did in some other life God should punish her by giving her a man like my father to marry," forty-three-year-old Basil Claddy told me once.

And thirty-seven-year-old Jimmy Dugan said, "Pa used to try to tell my mother he couldn't help it because we were so poor, but Ma said he could help it all right if he cared about her or us kids. She didn't hate him for what he done to her, she didn't care if she didn't have things for herself, she only wanted them for us kids and specially for me. A couple of times he knocked her down when she told him she hated him. If I'd been bigger, I'd have killed the bum."

Most Rowers say their mothers didn't speak out against their fathers the way Jimmy Dugan's mother did. They weren't that strong. Their husbands intimidated them and the women didn't put it past the men to slap them around, so they hid the contempt they felt for them. But not from their sons and especially not from these dearly beloved ones.

"I could always tell what was in my mother," forty-three-year-old Jake Reager says. "Most times she didn't talk out about what a louse my old man was. All she done was look and I knew how she felt inside of her. Sometimes she used to say to me, 'Sonny, dear, you grow up to be like your pa and what good'll my whole life be then? I'll only be sorry I lived.' I promised her I wouldn't but

49

still and all I was so a-scared I might grow up to be like him."

I met many men along Skid Row, U.S.A., who were suffering with the recognition that the seed of their fathers was in them.

Not all the beloved sons along Skid Row, U.S.A., are victims of such complicated relationships between their parents. Some are only victims of their mothers' overwhelming love. Their mothers always treated them like kings.

You look at them today, matted hair no comb has run through for months, bleary eyes and mottled skin from all the sneaky in them, humpbacked stance affected even by the straight-bodied ones around here, and you just can't believe that anyone ever could have doted on these. Their mothers did though. And how they did. The men tell you about how excruciatingly much their mothers cared about them. ("Ma never thought about nobody else but me. Not Pa nor the other kids. Never gave no hoot in hell for nobody else.") They sound proud while they talk to you about their mothers' love, but their pride when you examine it carefully is not unmixed with anguish. For much as their mothers' love means to them, they still do not respect it. Many of them never did respect it, not even when they were little.

Few of the men who hit Skid Row were ever outstanding children. On the contrary, many of them were neither as strong nor as bright as other children around them were. And still their mothers behaved as though they were stronger and smarter than everybody else. Naturally the children wanted to believe their mothers, not just because they wished they were as strong and smart as their mothers said they were, but more than that because they needed to believe in their mothers being right—when you're a child and can't believe in your mother's right and your mother is all you have in the world, what *can* you believe in then? So you've got to know whether your mother was right or not.

That question still plagues many Rowers from thirty to sixty years old but as close to childhood as though they were wearing rompers today. Once they trust you, they try to get you to answer their question. Were their mothers really right about them, or could they have been wrong? And if they were right, why is it that the men themselves are bums today instead of the lawyers and doctors their mothers willed them to be?

Cockeye Gross, a small man in his forties who always makes a point of keeping his crossed eyes half closed, told me, "My ma always wanted me to be a big lawyer. But then she died and never got to make me one."

I said, "Suppose she hadn't died, Cockeye?"

He was silent for a minute. Then he said, "Oh." Just that word. "She might have made a lawyer out of me," he said. "She was so good. She always hit the kids who called me Cockeye. She had a lot of trouble with some of their mothers who didn't like her hitting their kids. She always told them off. She used to say, 'Well, I don't like your kids calling my son Cockeye neither.' She used to say my

51

eyes were just beautiful." He smiled. "Yeah, just beautiful. But, sometimes I looked in the mirror and she made me so mad. My cockeyed eyes were homely. What'd she have to say they were beautiful for? I don't mean she was a liar. Ma'd tear her tongue out before she told a lie. Sometimes I didn't know if she *knew* I was cockeyed or not. If not, then how come? She was a smart lady. Everybody else knew. Little kids. The same way she always told me I was smart. But I was dumb. Everybody knew I was. But not my ma. Why not?"

In so far as she was able, Cockeye's mother dealt with his nagging doubts by keeping him insulated from the hostile world outside his home. No friendships with boys who might hurt his feelings, and when he grew older no friendships with girls who might. He quit school at sixteen. Not that he'd attended much before he quit either. The truant officer had been a regular visitor at his home from the time Cockeye began to go to elementary school, but his mother didn't mind. She used to stand right up to the truant officer and tell him that everybody in school picked on her son, the teachers expecting him to study too hard and the other kids making fun of him because they were jealous. Cockeye's father sometimes became angry when the truant officer came, but his mother could be depended upon to handle *him*.

When Cockeye was seventeen he got a job in a neighborhood garage working for "a dirty bum" named Cinelli. He was fired after six months.

"My ma was glad old Cinelli fired me. She said, 'You

got too good a disposition, sonny. You let Cinelli take advantage of you. I'm glad you got fired.' "

Cockeye got another job in another garage. His mother thought he was being overworked there too. He was fired again. His mother was pleased.

"I guess I must have had about six jobs altogether till Ma died and I left home because I couldn't stand the house without her. Every room I went in reminded me of her and I was always crying."

"How old were you when she died, Cockeye?" I asked.

"Twenty-two years," he said.

Nothing went right for Cockeye after he left home. He got jobs in other garages and was fired out of all of them. Then he tried to do factory work, but he was never fast enough to suit the bosses or to keep up with the other workers, so he got fired out of the factories too. He doesn't remember exactly when he hit Skid Row, but he thinks it must have been three or four years after he left home the first time.

"I got to Vine in Philadelphia. Then I stayed there because the flops and greasies was so cheap and there was nothing else I could do. I met some fellows got me in on dishwashing jobs. I still wash dishes when I get broke sometimes but I don't like to. The hot water and soap hurts my hands."

I once asked Cockeye Gross if he ever expected to leave Skid Row.

He looked at me a long time. "No."

"Why, Cockeye?"

"Because."

"Because why?"

"Just because."

"Because is no reason, Cockeye."

"It's all the reason I got."

I said, "Cockeye, do you want to get out?"

"Yeah," he said, "but I won't."

Actually, Cockeye Gross doesn't really want to leave Skid Row, U.S.A. Now that his mother is dead, it is a logical place for him to be. He can live here without any real struggle, just as he was able to live in his mother's home. He can always find some institution which will take care of his basic needs and ask nothing beyond what his mother used to ask in return—merely that he continue to be. The soup kitchens and the mission beds are all on Skid Row to oblige him, and the doorway companionship is available for the taking. Everything for free the way his mother used to arrange it.

Which is not to say that Cockeye does not hate and fear the world of Skid Row, U.S.A. But he is accustomed to living with fear and hate. And he knows that now that his mother is dead, fear and hate would be his lot no matter where he lived.

Naturally, Cockeye doesn't believe that Skid Row approximates the world his mother once made for him. He thinks he is here because he is an alcoholic.

"The whisky," he says, when you ask him why he is here. "I just can't leave it alone, see? I got the habit."

But, Cockeye Gross never took a drink before he hit

Skid Row. From what I have come to know about him, I don't believe he ever would have drunk if he hadn't come here where, if you're sober, you're antisocial. Cock-eye drinks heavily, not because he is driven by what he terms "the habit," but rather because that is the way along Skid Row, U.S.A.

3. The Whisky! The Whisky!

Actually, the majority of men along Skid Row, U.S.A., drink heavily because heavy drinking is the pattern of their world. Basically, they are men without egos, not addictive alcoholics. They are on Skid Row because they feel they belong there, and they drink because all their companions do. They are mistaking the effect for the cause when they say they are on Skid Row merely because they drink, and they are not the only ones who do it.

For many years, objective observers who have investigated Skid Row, U.S.A., have designated Rowers as hopeless alcoholics, and the few treatment programs that have been undertaken have been planned around that designation. No wonder they have been almost universally unsuccessful. You can't cure egoless men by treating them as though they were alcoholics any more than you can cure cancer patients by treating them as though they had heart trouble.

The real alcoholics who have been driven here by their

*addictions are a small minority along Skid Row, U.S.A.
You will have a hard time finding them. You often lose
them in the vast shuffle of egoless men when you do find
them. There is no outward distinction between them and
the egoless ones. They are just as hopeless about themselves and just as sure as the others that they won't leave
Skid Row till they die. They are just as sick. In some ways
they are sicker than the egoless ones are. They suffer more
consciously. Their feelings are not so blunted yet, and
they drink to help hasten the process.*

Mark Keller was the first Skid Rower I met who was
conscious of the difference between drunks and other Skid
Rowers. Dr. Mark Keller, Ph.D., Phi Beta Kappa, onetime
professor of English in a Midwestern university, and
Bowery habitué for the past nine years.

He is a small, slender man in his early fifties, with deli-
cate hands and feet. He has sandy blond hair and wide
blue eyes, which give him a helpless, little-boy kind of
look. His face is covered with ugly red sores. He wears a
blue shirt with three buttons missing and gray walking
shorts with holes in them. Instead of a belt, he wears a
string around the shorts. His Phi Beta Kappa key dangles
from the center of the string.

"I couldn't have stood it if this had been taken from
me," he said, pointing to the key. "Isn't it funny what
happens to people? I lost everything I ever had in my life
and accepted the losses with equanimity. If I had lost this
though," he fingered the Phi Beta Kappa key lovingly, "I

think I wouldn't have wanted to live any more. How ridiculous when everything else I had was sold within three months after I hit the Row. A good overcoat, two suits, brand new shoes, Chinese silk underpants, quite an indulgence, those—even two pairs of glasses I had, one for reading, one for ordinary use. There was one other thing I didn't sell. Don't ask me why. If there is any reason, I don't know it." He pulled a gray fedora hat out from under his left arm.

Some weeks after I first met him, I saw Mark Keller trying to sell his fedora hat on Rivington Street. That is the Bowery block known as the "fleamarket" to its habitués who buy and sell things there.

Dr. Keller was very drunk the day I saw him. He talked to a youngish roly-poly man who kept rubbing his stomach while he bargained.

"Here's a lovely hat," Dr. Keller said. "I could be induced to sell it to you. Provided that you ask me properly. You see, I like your face, otherwise nobody could prevail upon me to sell this hat to you."

The roly-poly man examined the hat. He returned it to Dr. Keller. "Junk," he said.

Dr. Keller said, "A lovely hat. A beautiful hat. A hat to grace the head of kings."

The roly-poly man rubbed his stomach. "Greasy as a stinkpot," he said.

"Grease can be removed."

"Junk."

"A beautiful, beautiful hat. Useful for preserving man's dignity."

"Who needs a hat in the summer anyways?"

"But, my dear man, think ahead. There is an old proverb, Irish, I believe. 'When summer is here, winter can't be but around the corner. 'Tis well for squirrels to gather their nuts while they may.' You know the little pig who had his house blown down? Why? Because he was unprepared. Take a lesson from that little pig, my good friend. Do not let winter catch *you* unawares."

The roly-poly man stuck his hand out again for the hat. "Let me look at the piece of junk again."

"Sticks and stones will break my bones," Keller said, "but names—can hurt me too. As the old saying goes, a proverb, my friend, a Scotch proverb really, 'Love me, love my hat.' That's what I was always telling my wife. 'Bettina,' I used to say to her, Betty Jane was her name, but she always insisted we call her Bettina, 'Bettina,' I used to say, Scotch proverb, 'love me.'"

The roly-poly man returned the hat. "It stinks."

"Language, my good man." Keller smiled tolerantly. He put his hands on his hips. "Can you read, my friend?"

"Yeah," the roly-poly man said, "sure. I can punch you in the nose." He made a lunge for Keller. He missed him.

"If you can read, little man," Keller placed the hat so that the label showed, "there is no need for me to tell you that this hat comes from Saks Fifth Avenue."

The roly-poly man said, "Poo."

"Thirty-five cents is all I want from you," Keller said.

He smiled, patted himself on the shoulder tolerantly, as though he was patting a child. "Well, I guess not. It is man's intelligence that distinguishes him from beasts. So, I know you don't want to buy my hat, not for thirty-five dollars or thirty-five cents or three cents and five mills. What do you want to buy? My friend. What do I have that intrigues you? And what little sum will you offer? Buy my shirt, my pants, my genuine English walking shorts? Buy my love, my light?"

The roly-poly man looked Keller over, up and down, up and down.

"Buy my love, my light, my walking shorts?" Keller asked.

The roly-poly man went up close to Keller. He put a short, fat hand on the string around the English walking shorts. He flipped the string.

Keller smiled. "Do not leave me exposed to a universe that cares not a whit in hell for me and mine."

The roly-poly man went on flipping the string. He touched the Phi Beta Kappa key. "Well, you can sell me that."

Keller looked at the key. He kept on looking down on it.

"I'll give you thirty-five cents for *that*."

"Thirty-five cents for learning. Reward for knowledge, Bettina love."

"Fifty cents." The roly-poly man rubbed his stomach. "Take it or leave it, you crazy galoot."

"We're going up now, Bettina. Fifty beautiful cents. Five small wines for knowledge. If only this were depression instead of prosperity, fifty cents could buy ten small wines, my darling, my lover, my sweet."

"Well, what do you say?"

Keller put his hand around the Phi Beta Kappa key. He fingered it gently.

"Well?"

Keller kept fingering the key.

"I ain't got all day. Make up your mind. Take it or leave it."

Keller looked up at the roly-poly man. He didn't say anything.

The roly-poly man said, "crazy galoot." He smiled and walked away.

Keller watched him go. He watched him for three blocks, weaving in and out. Then he said in a quiet voice, "Come back, come back, mister. You've got yourself a sale." He turned and began to walk as fast as his unsteady feet would carry him, in the opposite direction from the roly-poly man.

I learned Mark Keller's background. I met his wife Betty Jane and his nineteen-year-old daughter Anita. They are both attractive women, dark-haired and dark-eyed. They share a five-room apartment on Riverside Drive in New York. Anita goes to college. Betty Jane works as an advertising copy writer for a large downtown firm.

"It's so good of you to be interested in Daddy," Anita said. "Mummy and I are happy to hear anything about him. He won't let us see him. We went down to that——" She stopped.

"You can say it out, darling," her mother said. "We went to the flophouse Mark lives in and begged the man in the cage to get him to come out to see us. He wouldn't come, just told the man he didn't want to see us. He said he'd put us both out of his life."

Mrs. Keller said that she and Mark had been married twenty-three years ago.

"I once thought we had a good marriage. I always tried to please Mark. I used to think he was pleased. Well, as pleased as someone like Mark could be. I remember when we were first married he told me that no one had ever loved him enough. He said, 'You must love me more than everyone else put together.' He frightened me. I used to sit alone and wonder how I could love him as much as he wanted me to. I used to beg God to make me a big enough person."

Mark Keller achieved his university instructorship soon after he married. Betty Jane says that the head of his department respected him and that he received the usual promotions and seemed slated for a full professorship.

"Sometimes, I think I must have been very stupid in those days." She kept fiddling with the narrow silver marriage band which she still wears. "Now, I know how he was. But then, right up until the time he began to drink so much, I thought he was—well, not unhappy, quite well-satisfied with his job, you know."

"Poor Mummy," Anita said, "you thought he was quite well-satisfied with you too."

"Not exactly," Betty Jane shook her head at her daughter. "Not exactly."

Anita said, "One night I'll never forget. I must have been around eleven then. Daddy came home drunk. He started yelling at Mummy. 'Commonplace, am I? Casper Milquetoast, hunh? I'll kill you if you call me names again.' I remember Mummy's face then. She was more surprised than scared. She said, 'I never called you a name in my life.' I said, 'Daddy.' I had come out of bed, you see, and was standing in my nightgown. It was flannel and it had daisies on. Daddy had bought it for me. 'Please don't yell at Mummy,' I said. Then he punched me in the nose. It began to bleed. Mummy screamed. I didn't want to cry. But I couldn't help myself. Daddy stood and watched us both. He laughed. Then he took a knife and started running after Mummy with it. He said, 'You'll never think I'm commonplace again.'"

Mark Keller's recollection of the evening he made his daughter's nose bleed and threatened his wife with a knife is as keen as Anita's. And he is eaten up alive by his guilt. He talks about that time in his sober moments, and the self-hatred which the recollection elicits in him is a horrible thing to watch. You sit beside Mark Keller, you listen to him talk about his wife and his daughter and you realize no punishment anyone could devise for him could ever be more devastating than the one he has already devised for himself. Sometimes he sits and knocks his head against a wooden table over and over again. He knocks it hard. "Mark," you say, "look, Mark, sure what

THE WHISKY! THE WHISKY!

you did to Anita and Betty Jane was terribly wrong. But
listen, Mark, we all do things. Try to forget about that
night. Forgive yourself. Anita and Betty Jane already have
forgiven you."

Mark Keller looks at you.

"I ought to gouge my eyes out," he says.

I told that to Betty Jane. "Mark says he ought to gouge
his eyes out."

She answered, "Dear God! That's the kind of man he
is. I never knew what he was. Isn't it strange to live your
life right alongside of another person, think you're sharing
his thoughts and moods and still not have the remotest
idea of what he's feeling?" She rested her head on her
hands. "Poor Mark was a driven man. He took a Ph.D.
degree when he was forty-three. At first, I thought he was
taking it for the usual reasons, oh, professional advance-
ment at the university, the pleasure of learning, anything
like that. It wasn't till he was on one of his drinking sprees
that he let me know the truth. He was taking the degree
just to show all of us. He had a terrible urge to perfection.
I used to plead with him. 'Mark, you'll drive yourself
crazy. Relax.' He always laughed at me. 'God, the things
you don't know,' he used to say, 'the wonderful things
I am and aim to be. *I am a lover.*' When he got into his
moods he accused me of every crime in the book. He
would use the most vulgar language to me. He said that
I did not know how to arouse a man's love, that I was the
kind of a woman who went around perverting little boys.
'The only thing I'm happy about,' he used to say, 'is that

I never gave you a son to use for your dirty schemes.' He used to describe his own imaginary love affairs to me. According to him, all my dearest friends had offered themselves to him. Some he turned down, some he accepted, 'on my own terms,' he used to say. He would describe the kind of relations he had with them until he turned my stomach and I screamed at him to stop. One time he said to me, 'Do you think sex comes for nothing? All these years I've been giving you too much for too little.'"

Mark Keller's addiction to alcohol developed over a period of years. He started out as a social drinker, or at least that's what people conceived him to be. Today, during the few times when you catch him sober and objective, he says, "Underneath I really knew all the time that I was not a social drinker. I always needed liquor so much. I used to drink more than other people at parties. Betty Jane could always hold her liquor, but she would stop at two or three. Other people would drink four or five. But I'd have to go on and on. I didn't want to. I couldn't help myself. Everything that happened in my life was reason for me to drink. If I was sad, several cocktails would make me feel better. If I was happy, I had to celebrate my happiness."

Mark Keller says that he felt like a great man during most of the early years of his drinking. He rarely had hang-overs. He was able to tell himself that he drank because he wanted to, not because he had to, and that he could stop any time.

He discovered he couldn't stop though, and there were

times after those first years when he wanted to—desperately. Those were the times when he had a hard time holding on to his job, and Betty Jane, distraught, threatened that this was the last time—one more binge, she said, and she would pick up Anita and leave him. Those were the times when he begged Betty Jane to stay and threatened to kill himself if she left him and took his baby away. What would be the use of living then? Then Betty Jane usually said something like, "Look, Mark, we want you too. Anita and I need you as much as you need us. Only how can we have each other when you're like this so much of the time?" The argument often ended with both of them crying and Mark's head held against Betty Jane's breast and Betty Jane stroking his head as she used to do to her daughter when she was a baby and unhappy.

"My darling," Mark used to begin those days, "forgive me. I love you. I'll never have another drink again. I promise you. If I break my promise this time, you can leave me. You know I won't break it now, darling."

And the frantic attempts to keep his promise, to hold his wife and daughter and job. And the contempt and self-hatred in him when he could not keep his promise. And the first drink just to eliminate the contempt, just to help him to deal with the self-hatred. I'll stop after the first one. He was not fooling anybody though. Underneath all the rationalizing, he knew that there would be a second drink after the first and so on and on to hell with Betty Jane.

Mark first began to experience the terror of real alcoholic hang-overs during the twelfth year of his drinking.

"I want to kill myself when I get a hang-over," he says. "I can't get up from my bed. Every part of my body aches. There is a garbage taste in my mouth. My ears are stuffy. I can't open my eyes. And the dizziness, oh God, the dizziness. I can't stand. I can't sit. I can't even lie flat. But I have to do something, so I lie flat. And I become terribly fearful. I worry about dying or going insane. I can only fight the feeling with more whisky."

Mark Keller seeks oblivion from liquor, not a lift any longer. His whole life is built around the bottle.

"Whisky can give you a lift," he says, "but I can't afford whisky any more. The things I can afford to drink don't lift me. They make me numb. I drink sneaky pete all the time when I can afford it. When I can't I drink pink ladies. Have you ever tasted pink ladies, bums' way? Well, let me tell you how to prepare them. After all, you may have some fancy guests you'll want to impress some day. Give me a small credit line when you serve it though. Smile prettily at your guests and say, 'And now I want to introduce you to Dr. Keller the wino's own inimitable pink lady. Draw up close and I'll show you how it's done!' Then, you merely squeeze alcohol out of pink wax and add water to it. It may leave your fingers a little pink, of course, but what's a little coloring among friends?"

Mark Keller tries to smile. It doesn't quite come off. He places a shaking hand on his head. He shakes it off again.

He looks at you, straight at you, with eyes boring into yours. They are dead eyes.

"And perhaps you'd appreciate learning to make another unusual drink," he says. "My friends and I call it the 'white elephant.' Unique name, that, isn't it? To make, take one part wine, one part bay rum, and mix the two together. Very delicious really, oh a truly delectable drink, my dear."

He laughed and laughed, soundlessly but so hard that the tears fell down his face.

"I know some of the most unusual drinks on God's green earth, black shoe polish for one. I stole some once at a mission flop. I was desperate to get the coloring out so I looked all over for a piece of cloth to strain it through. A slice of bread would have done as well. But, as you have doubtless discovered for yourself, 'Man only proposes. God disposes.' I could find neither bread nor cloth. So, I drank the polish with all the black. The color ran out of my mouth and down onto my neck. I left it there for a week. I owned a cracked pocket mirror in those days. I used to look into it practically every hour on the hour."

Why did Mark Keller, a man such as he was, end up on Skid Row?

His father-in-law says, "Why? I'll tell you why. Because Mark's a weakling and always was."

Mark's mother-in-law echoes what her husband has said. "Mark never did have much will power. Just couldn't muster up enough will power to stop that habit from getting hold of him."

Mark Keller's own mother says, "Betty Jane forced my boy to drink. She used to drive him, always wanting more money than a college professor could earn. She didn't care about making him stop either. After he began drinking, she still permitted liquor around the house."

Mark Keller's father blames his wife. "Rita always spoiled that boy, pampered and pampered him, until I used to tell her, 'You'd better look out.'"

A law student who dates Mark's daughter, Anita, knows exactly what's been driving Mark. "That awful old urge to destruction," he says with the frightening assurance of the very young.

Betty Jane says, "If he wouldn't stop for my sake, I thought he might for Anita's. He just didn't love us enough, I guess." In another mood, she says, "If only I had been more understanding of Mark, perhaps I could have made him stop."

Mark and Betty Jane's family doctor, an old beau of Mark's mother, says, "What's the matter with people anyway? Why do they keep talking of will power and love and urge to destruction? Why can't they learn once and for all that Mark Keller is a sick man? All alcoholics are sick men."

The doctor's viewpoint is not new or startling. Modern scientific research on alcoholism, badly hampered by inadequate financing though it is, has disclosed, once and for all, that we must throw aside the oversimplified notion that any one particular external factor can be the cause of alcoholism and that its removal will automatically solve the problem. They have studied alcoholics physiologically, psychologically, and as products of their environments. To some extent they have disagreed with one another.

There are scientists and practicing physicians who believe that alcoholism is completely physiological in origin. There are other doctors, particularly psychiatrists, who are equally certain that the origins are entirely psychological. And there are many workers in the field who have come to believe that the answer may be found somewhere in the middle. Only time and more research will prove which views are correct. One thing they have all said, however, strongly and unmistakably: alcoholism is a disease and alcoholics must be helped—not blamed or ridiculed. They have defined the alcoholic as a person who has an uncontrollable craving for alcohol. Sometimes the craving is obvious when alcoholics first take liquor. More often it develops slowly and progressively. But however the drinking starts, it ends up as a compulsive drive that cannot be denied.

Most Skid Rowers can plan their drinking, while true alcoholics, whether on the Row or off it, cannot begin to do so.

Dr. Robert Straus, formerly Director of the Yale University School of Alcohol Studies, makes this point in his book *Mental Health and Mental Disorder*. Referring to four groups of homeless men whom he and his staff studied in New York City and in New Haven, Connecticut, he said, "It was possible to label 80 to 90 per cent habitual, symptomatic excessive drinkers rather than addictive alcoholics because they place their greatest emphasis on the duration of their drinking rather than on its intensity. They appear to be seeking a plateau. Given a five-dollar bill these men would not be likely to think how quickly they could achieve a state of peak intoxication but instead would plan their drinking so they could maintain a limited level of effect from alcohol for as long a period of time as possible."

Mark Keller was certainly never able to plan his drinking. His trouble lay in the fact that, until he reached bottom, "became a Bowery bum," as he says, he always thought he could plan.

"Not that knowing that I can't makes an iota of difference now," he says. "I know I can't control myself and I hate myself for being a weakling but I go on drinking all the same."

A fifty-three-year-old Chicago lawyer named Bud Roberts echoed everything Mark Keller said about the self-hatred and the lack of control of true addictive alcoholics.

"God," he says, "if I could only make somebody understand how I hate the stuff. When I tell people, they always say, 'If you hate it so, why don't you quit it?' If I only could. People say, 'When you have your happy times while you're under the influence, try and think how awful you'll feel when you're sober.' To an alkie like me, that's a real laugh. Happy times. What happy times? There aren't any, any more. When I first started to drink there were good moments, but not now. I can't even recall them. No. I don't drink for the good moments any more. None of us bums do. Now, I drink to run away from the pain. My life is a series of drowsings and wakings all day and all night. I never sleep through a night and wake up refreshed in the morning like other people do. I drowse and then I wake up with a heavy head. I can't get it off the pillow. I'm so dizzy and nauseous. So I do the only thing I know to help myself. I take a drink the minute I get up. Sometimes, fresh drinks won't stay down though. I wish I could die then. Because, you know, when an alkie takes a drink it can sometimes help him overcome the shakes. But if you can't keep a drink down, then how are you going to help the shakes? Nobody who hasn't got the shakes can know how they feel. You don't feel like a human being any more. I shake so badly sometimes that I can't stand or pull on my pants. Sometimes, I can't even hold my bottle."

Bud Roberts looks more like seventy-three than fifty-three. He is close to six feet tall, but he stoops, so that he appears much shorter than he is. He cuts his ample, prematurely white hair himself, short, so that he can avoid flophouse head lice. He has been on the Row for eleven years now, and he has experienced everything that other Rowers have—hospitalization for delirium tremens, the jail drunk tank, everything.

"Sometimes I wonder at how society can be so cruel as it is to men like me. I get drunk and I need help. So they pick me up and throw me into jail. What good does it do me to be locked up? Certainly I'm off liquor while I'm in jail. But they have to let me out again, and then I'm bound to go back on. I've been in jail sixty times off and on since I became a bum. Not just here in Chicago. All over the country. What an experience jail's been for me. Most places they threw me in a drunk tank with a bunch of other poor drunks. I think drunk tanks are disgraces to this country. We're supposed to be enlightened, aren't we?

"I want to tell you an experience I had in a drunk tank once. I don't even remember the name of the town I was in, but the name doesn't really matter, one town's tank is like any other town's. A cop threw me in this particular tank with stone walls and stone floors and no facilities whatever, neither heat nor electricity nor toilet facilities. It happened to be midwinter. About forty men were lying on the floor, just shivering and trying to sleep. I lay down too and tried to sleep. But just as I was falling asleep I was awakened by a terrible sound. A great big fat man was beating the air and talking into the atmosphere. I still remember every word he said as though I'd heard him yesterday. 'Stop screamin', ya goddamn stinkin' son of a bitch train. I'll bust ya one, ya say that again. Stop. Stop. Goddamn ya. Drop dead, train.' Then he fell down. He put his hand in front of his eyes. 'Don't do it, train.' Then he sat up and he said, 'Ya didn't have to run me over. But I knew you was a-going to. I knew it.' Poor fellow, he had the d.t.'s awfully bad that night."

I said, "He should have been in a hospital, not in jail."

Bud Roberts nodded. "Should've been but wasn't. Plenty of towns throw you into drunk tanks if you've got d.t.'s. They say the hospitals don't have room for bums, not even sick ones. Of course, big cities like Chicago, New York, and Philadelphia aren't like that. Their hospitals take drunks if they have d.t.'s. But you've got to have d.t.'s though. They have no room to take you for anything less."

Bud Roberts learned that the hard way. Several times when he felt ill, "on my last leg," he put it, he'd tried to get himself admitted to municipal hospitals.

But the admitting officers had made short shrift of him. "This hospital is for sick people," they'd told him. "We've got no room for drunks."

A couple of times Bud had countered with "All right, I'm a drunk. I'm not saying I'm not. But I'm sick as well as drunk. Can't you see?" And when he learned that his arguments availed him nothing, he developed a technique for dealing with disapproving hospital admissions officers.

"I learned to simulate the effects of delirium tremens," he said. "It isn't too difficult for someone who's been there before. I find a policeman, or if there isn't one around as is often the case, for we aren't overpoliced in our part of the town, I send a friend to find one. Then, when a policeman is in sight I yell, scream, throw my arms around, and make believe I'm seeing pink elephants or monkeys who are banging piano keys. I've seen those sights often enough so I'm very good at describing them to policemen. I always get taken to the hospital."

"What happens after you get to the hospital?" I asked.

Bud Roberts shrugged. "Nothing much. They give me a bed in a psycho ward. It isn't very pleasant there but

75

what the hell? Who am I to kick? And before I'm there too long, I always get some 'stuff.'"

"Stuff?" I asked.

He smiled. "Paraldehyde to you. I love it. It's foul but I love it. It has a wonderful effect. It makes your head stop throbbing and your shakes let up. It makes you feel like a new man."

"Then what?" I asked.

"Then you stay in the hospital for three days sleeping in a real bed and eating real food. You get to feeling stronger so's you're ready for a brand new bout by the time they kick you out. Of course, sometimes things don't work out that well. A man comes in with the real d.t.'s, he can be pretty violent and so they'll put him in a strait jacket and give him other drugs instead of the 'stuff.' Time he's ready for out, he still feels like hell."

"Bud," I asked, "have you ever left a hospital and then thought of yourself as ready to make a new start?"

"I guess not," he said. "I always knew better. I know my place, you see. I know what I am."

I said, "What are you?"

He smiled. "A drunk who has found my home at last."

Bud Roberts has a wife and three daughters. He has a nice home in Evanston, a suburb of Chicago. His family is willing to take him back, but Bud says he'll never go home again.

"I tried," he says, "three times. I went back home and got cleaned up and got some shots from our family doctor and started trying to live like a human being. Everybody tried *so* hard to help me. That was the trouble. They tried too hard. They treated me like a little boy. They always acted like they were walking on glass in my presence. Not just Marion and the three girls. The neighbors too. They'd talk to me in hushed voices and look at me as though I were an apparition instead of a person. 'And how are you feeling today, Mr. Roberts?' I hated to go outdoors. I was ashamed. People's kindness shamed me. I wanted to hit them for being so nice to me. I did hit my youngest daughter Joyce one time because she said, 'Daddy's been such a good man lately. He hasn't had a single thing to drink.' I beat her with my fists. Something in me wouldn't let me stop. My wife had to call the police. She refused to have me booked after they came though. I went on a binge to end all binges that night. I kept the whole neighborhood in an uproar. I wanted to beat everyone who came to our door because I considered them my enemies. My wife said, 'These are your friends, dear.' But I only laughed at her. I said, 'Friends? You call these my friends? You don't know friends from holes in the wall. Come on to the stem with me, if you want to meet my friends. I have a whole group of real friends at Bailey's flop.'"

Most addictive alcoholics I met along Skid Row, U.S.A., feel, as Bud Roberts does, that Skid Row habitués are the only real friends they have.

"A real friend should not look down on you," Bud says. "The only friends I have who don't look down on me are right here. I belong to a whole group of friends here, and

77

although they're not the best-educated men in the world, I thank God for them. They're kind and good, and they think as much about me as they do about themselves."

The group of "friends" Bud Roberts belongs to was organized on Chicago's main stem about two years ago. There are seven members, including Bud, who "stick together" and "work together" to secure their whisky.

Drinking groups like Bud Roberts's are all over Skid Row, U.S.A. Their members are known to Row habitués as "lushes" and are considered aristocrats, because they have friends and supporters and need never live in loneliness. They look down upon the other Rowers who are forced to live alone—"rubby-dubs" who drink raw alcohol and "winos" who exist on sneaky pete and "bums" who drink whatever they can get but always drink by themselves.

"Living with friends keeps you feeling better than you'd feel otherwise," Bud says. "You're not anxious as when you're all by yourself. You've got somebody else to live for when you're a lush. You're for everybody, not just yourself. My group shares everything. If you gave me three dollars now, I wouldn't keep it for myself. I'd contribute it to the kitty and share it with all my friends."

I said, "Does everybody contribute to the kitty?"

He said, "Of course."

I said, "What do you do with the money?"

He smiled. "The thing we're in business for. Buy whisky. What else?"

I said, "Suppose some other fellows don't have three dollars to contribute?"

"Their time will come," he said. "You'd be surprised at how well our co-operation works out in the long run. If I contribute more today, another boy's sure to contribute more tomorrow. Besides, how much you give becomes unimportant when you consider what you get."

"What do you get?" I asked.

"A feeling of safety and belonging," he said. "A feeling that you have friends who will help you when you're in need and not look down their noses the way your friends outside would. They'll take care of you when you're ill. I had pneumonia and the d.t.'s together one time. My wife Marion loves me, but I don't think she would have had the stomach to see me through that illness. My friends down here had the stomach. They kept me in the Golden Bough flop and took turns nursing me. They used to feed me their whisky. Their own whisky and believe me they wanted it badly. They almost went crazy without it. But still they gave it to me. Gave me their own whisky because I needed it worse. Can you imagine that? I don't think you can. Nobody in the world would have done that for me. Not my wife or my children or my so-called friends. Don't think I blame them. I really don't. How can they know what a man like me goes through when he needs a drink and can't get one? I don't blame them but I can't live with them either. Yes, this place is my home. It's hell but it's where I live."

4. Fifty-one Ain't Old in Russia!

Many Skid Rowers are men and women above middle years. Some are in their fifties and sixties, able-bodied and wanting to work instead of exist along Skid Row, but unable to get jobs. Unskilled workers all their lives, they have been discarded from their jobs, now that they have grown older, and have been replaced by younger, stronger men. They live in the flops and eat in the greasy spoons and support themselves by such jobs as dishwashing on occasion or working seasonally in summer resorts.

Many are sixty-five and older and are too feeble to care for themselves. Some of them beg for existence, sleeping and eating in the missions when they can and resting in alleys and doorways and scavenging garbage pails when they must. Some get old-age assistance and Social Security checks, ranging from forty to ninety dollars a month.

When I first met bull-faced Big Jackson, I considered him another alcoholic. I never saw him when he wasn't either drunk or panhandling for sneaky pete. He always seemed such an evil drunk.

I used to watch Jackson inveigle people into shaking hands with him.

"Come on, man." He used to stick out his big, red paw. "Shake." And he used to grip the hand of the man who was shaking with him and hold on, squeezing it until the other man winced. Then Jackson would smile to show beige-brown, strong-looking teeth. "Hey, man, I said shake."

When the man screamed with pain, only then would Jackson release him. "Whatsa matter anyways?" he'd ask. "Man, man, don't tell me I hurt you. How come? I can't hurt you. I can't hurt no fly. I'm fifty-five years, too old and weak to keep a job. How can I hurt you?"

Big Jackson was a trucker before he became a Skid Rower. He'd been a loader for various firms.

"I begun loading trucks at thirteen," he tells. "I wasn't a smart kid in school so I quit and begun working with my old man. He used to be the best loader in the whole business. I come close to being second best. I got a muscle when I was thirteen that most guys of twenty-five would be proud if it was on them. Every time my old lady used to invite some of her lady friends, she used to say to me, 'Hon, make a muscle for my friends.'"

Big Jackson's father dropped dead of a heart attack when he was fifteen, and Jackson assumed the support of his widowed mother.

"I was very proud to be able to take care of my ma myself. I knew most boys my age wouldn't have been able to do it. Their mothers would've had to go on charity. But I kept getting better and better on the job. I don't mean to boast but I got a reputation in the business. All the bosses wanted me. I never had to take nothing off of any of them."

Until he came into his forties, Big Jackson lived with the illusion that strength was perpetual power and he was strength. He quit jobs and took new ones as the mood moved him.

"Ma and me used to laugh our heads off every time I quit a job. I'd come home and tell her I had a fight with the boss and told him he should go take a jump in the lake! Ma'd say, 'Fine, fine!' I always got a better job the next day."

During the year Big Jackson got to be forty-seven years old, his mother gave him his first feeling of work insecurity. He came home early one Wednesday afternoon, disheveled but triumphant.

"That bum," he said.

"Who?" his mother asked.

Jackson said, "I bashed that boss's face in for him."

His mother didn't smile. She only peered at him through nearsighted eyes in horn-rimmed glasses.

"I bashed his dopey face in," Big Jackson repeated.

His mother removed the apron from around her ample middle. "Why?"

"Why what?"

"Why'd you have to go'n do it?"

"The dumb rat says to me, 'Jackson, you ain't so hot as you think you are.' I says to him, 'Oh, I ain't, ain't I?' He says to me, 'No. Goddamn it, Jackson, you ain't.' I told him, Ma, I says, 'You better take that back, mug.' He says, 'I ain't taking nothing back. I'm the boss of this here outfit.' I says to him, 'You ain't my boss.' Then I let him have it right between the eyes."

His mother said, "What's about the job, son?"

"Plenty others where that comes from," Big Jackson said. But he felt the first stirring of fear in him. He knew that other men in his business were afraid. They often discussed their fears. "All the work you want when you're young. But when you get older, the boss'll kick you out." Well, let those other men talk. That kind of thinking was all right for those mediocre loaders. But it was all wrong for the second best loader in the whole business. Forty-seven or fifty-seven, he could get a job any time he wanted. Plenty of them around for the likes of him.

Big Jackson found out that jobs were not as plentiful for men of forty-seven as they were for men of twenty-seven. He applied for several jobs and was turned down on all of them. The bosses said, "You're too old," and sometimes they laughed when he asked them to let him prove what he could do. Finally, at his mother's urging, he went back to the boss he'd fought with and ate humble pie. The boss said Jackson could have his old job back but things would have to be different.

"You ain't the kingpin any more," he said.

A few weeks after he'd been hired back under these

disagreeable circumstances, Big Jackson's old boss re-
tired and his young son took over. Big Jackson developed
a dislike for the son who used to come down and watch
the men load, just stand around in an expensive blue suit
and a stiff-collared shirt, smoking his pipe and watching
the loading.

One day he told the boss's son, "Whatsa matter, young
fella, ain't you got no better place to slum?"

The boss's son answered, "Watch your tongue, old
man."

"Old man." Big Jackson put up his fists the way he had
been wont to do in the good old days. "Old man. Call
me that again and I'll kick your teeth in."

The boss's son exhaled pipe smoke. "Old man," he said.

Big Jackson felt he hadn't any choice. He had to start
acting on his word. Three men, all younger than he was,
had to pull him off the boss's son. One tackled him around
the legs and got him on the ground. Another sat on his
chest.

"They went and called the police on me. I got stuck
in the hoosegow," he says.

Of course he could not go back to his old job after the
fight. So he tried to find other loading jobs. He went from
firm to firm. Some bosses refused to talk to him. They just
looked at him and decided he was too old. Some interviewed him, gave him forms to fill out, asked for all of his
qualifications, approved the qualifications as it were, said,
"Fine. You've had good experience." And then said,
"Sorry, bud. Can't use you. You're too old."

Big Jackson had to face facts. Now that he was forty-seven, the big man was just a little man, and the second best loader in the business couldn't get a job. It was unbelievable but true. He questioned personnel managers and small bosses who did their own hiring, "Look, what difference is age? I can work as good as anybody. Why don't you give me a chance to prove it?" He preached at the men who refused to hire him. "You can't tell me it's right. Guy works all his life since he's a kid thirteen years old. Then you treat him like garbage. Throw him in the ash can. It's not right."

Today, Big Jackson is a profoundly bitter man. "You know how I feel when they tell me I'm too old to work?" he says. "Like a kick in the belly. I want to work. I got to work. What do I do if I can't work, lay down and die?"

I met many unskilled workers along Skid Row, U.S.A., who have been discarded from their jobs long before they were ready to stop working. Most of them, unlike Big Jackson, did not consider themselves the best in their fields. They never did have the work security Big Jackson had in his younger days. Most of them expected, from the time they started working, that they would be occupational hazards some day. So it should have been easier for them to face their unemployment than it was for Big Jackson, but it wasn't.

Skinny Danny Millar, fifty-one years old with bright brown eyes and hands that are constantly clenched when he talks to you, said, "Yeah, all the time I was working on construction jobs for outfits wasn't unionized, I knew I'd get canned someday. I never had had training so I could be valuable on a job. Any little kid could do the jobs I did. You didn't have to have brains. I knew I'd get fired out of the construction business as soon as I got old. I used to try to save a little money for when it happened to me. But I couldn't. Never got enough pay to. I used to say I'd commit suicide when I got old and nobody wanted to hire me. Whoever thought it would happen this soon though? Hell, fifty-one years old. Fifty-one. Fifty-one ain't old."

I said, "Fifty-one's young, Danny."

He smiled. "Not in this country," he said. "If you get what I mean."

I said, "What do you mean?"

He said, "Fifty-one ain't old in Russia. That's because Russia loves the common people. She don't hate them the way America does." He smiled. "I love Russia. I wisht I could go and live there."

I said, "You don't know anything about Russia, Danny."

"I know plenty about America though," he said significantly. "I was born a worker. My people was workers and they couldn't afford to give me an education to make a grand man out of me. All right. All I wanted to do was work, but the bosses didn't give me a chance. Fifty-one years old and you're finished in America. Why are you? If I was in Russia they'd be letting me work!"

You see the industrial discards along Skid Row, U.S.A., hanging around the public parks and listening avidly to the soapbox orators. They boo all pro-American sentiments and applaud all anti-American ones. Although they have no actual connection with the Communist Party, they have adopted and memorized all the old-time, stereotyped, Communist phrases.

"Comes the revolution," they tell you mirthlessly, "the bosses'll eat mud, not me."

I tried to find out how many discarded workers there are along Skid Row, U.S.A., but I couldn't. No figures. One thing I know though—there are many more of them around than we think there are.

There are also many more people over sixty-five than we know about. They live in the flophouses and eat in the greasy spoons and drink in the bloody buckets. Because many have pensions they are sought-after members of lush groups. There are "all kinds types" of old people on Skid Row too. Some live there because they like it. Some hate it but feel they can't afford to live elsewhere.

Many people are on Skid Row temporarily while they await admission into old people's homes. But they have been a long time getting admitted. In New York City there are only about ninety-four voluntary homes and two public homes for the aged. They accommodate about twelve thousand people. And there are over half a million people who are sixty-five years and over. If anything, New York's facilities are superior to those of other places. Old-age home waiting lists are long and vacancies usually occur only upon the death of residents.

Mrs. Lilly Regan who lives on Second Street off the Bowery has been trying to gain admission to an old people's home for the past eight years. She is sixty-nine years old. She is a small, slender woman with bright blue eyes and completely white hair which she wears in a bun. She has no teeth now, and so she does not smile very often. Despite turned-at-the-heel shoes and shabby dresses, there is a dignity about her. She lives in a furnished room up four flights of stairs. The ceiling and walls are peeling. But Mrs. Regan has hung wine draperies with bright yellow flowers on the narrow window, and she has almost covered the wall with pictures of her girl and two boys. The girl as a baby, resting on a poodle rug, bare back side in the air. The girl at three or four, long curls, pinky finger in her mouth. Then at eleven or twelve, the hair in pigtails now, the eyes solemn. And the boys in sailor suits with Buster Brown haircuts.

"My beautiful baby Loretta," Mrs. Regan has written on the girl's latest picture. And on the boys' a dedication in small, almost illegible letters. "I'll always love you, children."

Mrs. Regan says she spends many happy hours looking at her pictures. "It's not such a bad way to be old when you can think back and know you raised three wonderful children," she says. "Plenty of people around here have no pictures to look at or children to think about. I'm a pretty lucky woman, I guess."

One of Mrs. Regan's friends, a sallow, bent old lady who goes by the name of Raving Rachel, laughs at Mrs. Regan's luck.

She says, "Lucky? Hoo, ha. Mine worst enemies should only be so lucky."

A fat Skid Row prostitute who calls herself Pretty Peg also laughs.

"Lilly Regan calls herself lucky because she got those kids. She really ain't got them when you come right down to it. She only thinks she has. Poor Lil. I was sitting in the Down Under one time drinking a little sneaky. I looked up and seen Lil by my table. I was surprised because she never used to drink. She hated walking by saloons when she first came here. So, when I looked up and seen her standing by my table, I thought I was good and gone. I said, 'Hiya, Lil.' She said, 'Hiya, Peg.' I told her things on the street was pretty good and asked her did she want I should buy her some sneaky. She said no but she sat down by me anyways. She said she just came to prove I was making a big mistake when I told her her kids was no good. She said, 'I want to read you a letter from my daughter Loretta. "Dear Mommy, please come home. We miss you. Please come home. We miss you."' She kept saying those words so much it got me disgusted. Besides I'm a girl is always looking for a laugh. So I told Lilly, 'All them fancy schools you sent Loretta to couldn't of did her so much good if she can't write a better letter than this.' Then I asked her to let me see the letter. She said no. I told her to come on. She still said no. So I grabbed it. I was awful sorry. You know what writing was on that letter? There wasn't no writing. I didn't know what to say to Lil, so I said, 'Today, you got to let me buy you some sneaky.' She said O.K. We been drinking together ever since."

Lilly Regan is ashamed of her drinking, but she is realist enough to know that it helps her face the life she is forced to lead down here, and her realism helps her to handle her conflict.

"I have no friends any more except the ones here," she said simply, when I asked her why she drank, "and I want to be in the bunch. All of them drink. Pretty Peg and them say I'm a stuck-up pig when I'm not drunk."

You talk to Mrs. Regan, grieving the way plenty of old parents who live in more reputable places do, over children who have no more place in their lives for her, and you can hardly believe that she is a Skid Row habitué. I told her straight out one day, "Mrs. Regan, of all the places in the world for a woman like you to be living——"

She smiled her rare smile, attempting to hide her toothlessness with a hand in front of her mouth.

"I guess you're right about that, Miss, only where else am I going to live on forty-seven dollars a month?"

Mrs. Regan used to be a laundress. When she was young and the children were babies, she took washing home. She didn't start working in commercial laundries until her children were old enough to be left alone.

"I always needed to work," she says. "My husband was nice, such a big, healthy man with red cheeks, but he didn't like work much. Sometimes he got very mad at me or the babies. He used to tell us he shouldn't have gotten tied down with us. I didn't mind his talking to me like that. It hurt me, but I was still able to take it with a smile. But I got too mad to smile when he talked bad to my babies. So one time I told him, 'I'm the one brings the money in this house. You're tying me and the children down, not the opposite way around. I don't want you talking to my children any more. Get out of here.' I missed him when he first went away because—well—I needed him at night. I made up my mind I was going to control myself for my children's sake. I guess my babies needed me worse than I needed any man. What kind of a mother would I be if they weren't most important to me? I soon stopped caring about my husband. I didn't have time to care. When you have to work on a job and raise your boys and girls, you get too busy to miss things like—that."

Lilly Regan says that her two boys are doctors now and that her daughter Loretta is married to a lawyer.

Her friends on the street laugh when she talks about her children's professions.

"Michael and Jimmy doctors?" Pretty Peg asks. "If that ain't a laugh. One time when Lil first came here she told me what they really was—no good bums used to hang around horse places. And that Loretta! She's some lawyer's wife! All she is is a salesgirl in a department store. She got a screwy idea she can marry a rich guy if she makes believe she's a lady. That's why she don't want to see Lil no more. But Lil's more a lady than she'll ever be. Lil's too good for around here. She was just dumb to give them kids everything she ever had. She should be where there's other nice dames like her. Maybe an old ladies' home or something. She'd love to be in one."

When I asked Lilly Regan about whether she would like to be in an old ladies' home, she shrugged her shoulders and said she didn't care one way or another, but something in her face belied what she said.

"Mrs. Regan," I said, "most old people's homes are in nice neighborhoods."

She said, "Yes." Very noncommittally.

I said, "You might find some of your kind of women there."

"My kind?" she said. "I drink sneaky right along with Peg and them."

I said, "If you weren't here, you wouldn't be drinking sneaky."

"Maybe not," she said, "maybe not." Then she looked away from me. "If I could only get in one of those homes. If I only could. Some people down here don't feel like me. They'd rather be free. I wouldn't. I'd rather be clean. I never felt clean since I got down here. I scrub myself, I scrub the room. Still and all, I'm dirty. I could get clean in an old-age home."

Mrs. Regan applied for admission to three homes for the aged some four and a half years ago.

"I used to keep waiting for the mailman at first," she says.

Pretty Peg says, "Yeah. Every day her heart got a little more broke."

And Raving Rachel asks, "How long can a person wait?"

"I'm not waiting any more," Mrs. Regan says. "I gave up. Besides I know a couple of people much worse off than I am. They ought to get into homes first. One man is nice but he isn't right in the head, and one lady's so crippled up with the rheumatism she can hardly move around, poor soul. They have no place to go either. They ought to get homes before me."

I met the man and the lady she was talking about.

The lady, a seventy-one-year-old named Lenore Flaherty, lay on a mattress on the floor of a cold-water room on West Third Street. She was paralyzed in both legs. When I asked her how she got around, she smiled and said her landlady helped take care of her.

"I pay her twenty-six dollars a month. Her name's Mrs. Berger and she treats me nice most of the time. But now she wants me to raise her to thirty-two dollars a month. She does for me. She'll come in the morning and help lift me and walk me to the toilet in the hall. She don't like doing it and I can't say I blame her. But most of the time she's pretty nice about it though. Only time she ever gets angry is when I got to go at night. I had to call her two nights ago. I said I was awful sorry to bother her but I didn't know what else I could do. She said I could go on the mattress. I felt so miserable. You better talk now. I'll cry if I talk some more. A lot of people used to come to see me and stopped. I guess I cried too much for them. I don't cry any more. I won't cry now." She looked away from me. "I can always stop fast if I do have to start in crying.

I won't annoy you if you stay a couple of minutes. Lilly knows, don't you?"

Mrs. Regan said, "Yes, dear."

"See?" Lenore Flaherty asked.

Mrs. Regan smiled. "She'd rather have company than eat, wouldn't you, dear?"

Lenore Flaherty nodded.

"She'd have plenty of company in an old ladies' home," Mrs. Regan told me.

"Lenore Flaherty smiled. "Maybe somebody in an old ladies' home would be glad to help me to the bathroom at night too if I could only stop myself from crying in their faces."

"You wouldn't cry in their faces if you was in an old ladies' home," Mrs. Regan said.

"No," Lenore Flaherty agreed. "I'd be too happy then."

It sounds strange to hear women talking so longingly about entering old people's homes—even in the sordidness of this environment it sounds strange.

"Don't you think Lenore deserves a home more than me?" Mrs. Regan asked. "Tell the truth now."

I said, "Both of you deserve a home."

She smiled. "Bellywop Monkeyface deserves one too. He's a little bit crazy."

I met Bellywop Monkeyface at Lil Regan's house. He is called Monkeyface because his face is small and wizened and brown and wrinkled and because when he cries, which he does often, he screws it up like a monkey. He is

95

called Bellywop because he often navigates on his hands and feet and stomach.

Bellywop Monkeyface is close to eighty years old and is beyond caring about old-age homes or anything. He has some friends who care, though, among them a flophouse keeper named Jay Renard who knew Bellywop for years, "long before he became a fruitcake," as he puts it.

"He come here to my flop about ten years ago," Mr. Renard says. "He was a nice old fellow that paid his bills and minded his own business. He always had a pleasant good morning for everybody. I used to like him a lot. Everybody did. He didn't turn nutty till a couple of years ago. I seen him start in going but I didn't like to admit it. I didn't want to kick him out of the flop. I felt too sorry for him. Besides, there's so many of them nuts around here, one don't make no difference so you notice it. Then, bingo, one day he told me I stole his clothes away. He kept on talking about some purple shirt he was supposed to have and said I took it off of him. At first, I begun laughing and trying to tell him what the hell'd I want his shirt for, a big, fat, two-hundred-pound fellow like me and him such a little guy? Besides I knew he never owned no purple shirt. He got mad at me and tried to burn my place down to get revenge. Some of the boys caught him in the toilet. I had to put him out, much as I hated to."

Bellywop Monkeyface is the proud owner of a pocket full of things—a piece of string, a lady's comb with most of its teeth missing, a sheet of crumpled newspaper. He once told me how he came to accumulate his treasures.

"I—count—men—I—see—spitting. I—get—a—hundred. Then—I go—around—corner. I—find something."

Bellywop's game reminded me of one I used to play when I was seven years old. I used to count things too, straw hats as it happened. I had the same faith in those days that Bellywop has today. I used to count seventy-five straw hats, and I also walked around the corner and found something, a stone, a piece of string.

I told Bellywop about that game when I was seven. He giggled.

"I—three—years—old," he told me.

Head hanging, feet dragging, he walked away. He talked while he walked. "I—three—years—old."

I didn't see Bellywop for many weeks. Then, when I did see him last, it was by accident, not design. He was standing in a tenement doorway, on a side street not too far from his usual hangout. A little girl with long black curls came out of the doorway. As soon as Bellywop saw her he began to breathe heavily. He exposed himself to her. She screamed and ran away. Bellywop shuffled after her but could not catch up.

Is there an answer to the problem of Lenore Flaherty or Mrs. Regan or all the other old people who live along Skid Row, U.S.A.? Certainly the answer is not in old people's homes as they are presently set up. For even if Lenore Flaherty had the ingenuity to make application for admission to a home for the aged, and most old people who are here on Skid Row are not independent enough to think in such terms, waiting lists are so long that admission when they need it would be a practical impossibility anyhow.

There seems to be no answer for Bellywop Monkeyface either—at least not so far. For with old-age homes being unable to accommodate even the normal aged, they cannot be expected to provide custodial care for the senile aged. And there are no other institutions set up to do so. Mental hospitals, overcrowded as they are, cannot assume responsibility for them either.

In December of 1954, New York's Supreme Court Justice Benjamin Brenner found himself "reluctantly forced to certify four homeless persons as mentally ill although they were not mentally ill in fact" because he could think of nothing else to do with them.

"The statute of the New York State Mental Hygiene Law," he said, "prohibits admission of any person to a mental hospital for any cause other than mental illness, and since denial of custodial care and hospitalization to these people would probably result in their death, I find myself compelled to certify them as mentally ill."

Justice Brenner described the four people involved in his opinion.

"One is a seventy-eight-year-old woman who has a permanent hip injury, is unable to walk, is overtalkative and almost blind. Another is a ninety-eight-year-old man who has suffered several strokes and loss of memory. The third is an eighty-four-year-old man whose senility is rapidly worsening. The fourth is a man of sixty-four who has speech difficulty."

Justice Brenner's action elicited widely contradictory feeling among the courts and social agencies of New York.

Miss Ollie A. Randall, a consultant on the aged for the Community Service Society termed the justice's act a "welcome shock." "He has," she said, "underscored a problem that deserves a high, if not the highest, priority in community planning."

Commissioner of Welfare Henry McCarthy was more critical than Miss Randall.

"I just can't believe that any responsible psychiatrist would recommend certification to the judge of a patient who wasn't actually a psychotic. If he does commit a person who is not psychotic to a state hospital, that state hospital upon examining the patient will send him right back home again."

Commissioner McCarthy is right, of course. State hospitals are not the place for people who merely need custodial care. But, so far, no other place is being provided for them either. New York City is considering a vast expansion program for the aged. It intends to begin at Ellis Island, until recently an immigration center.

"We want to create homesteads for aged men and women on the island," McCarthy says. "We can accommodate about two thousand old people."

Commissioner McCarthy knows that Ellis Island alone is not the answer. And he is continuing to campaign for more homes for the homeless aged.

In the meantime, in New York as elsewhere all over the country, old people, sane as well as senile, continue to live along Skid Row, U.S.A. Some of them hate it. Some start out hating it but end up adjusting. And a few actually prefer it to any other life.

There is a man named Martin Mack who flops in Chicago. He used to be an itinerant lecturer on biology. He is a small, soft-spoken man of seventy-one.

"When I first found myself here, I was ashamed every time I walked out of my flop," he said. "I thought I had nothing left to live for. I wanted to commit suicide. Once I thought the suicide idea through, though, I knew it was all wrong, because I really wanted to live. So I decided to learn to live here. I found the living very hard at first, but now I'm not sure I'd leave here if I got the chance. A couple of years ago, I would have been very pleased if I'd been able to get into an old people's home. But now I wouldn't enter one on a bet. I guess I'm beginning to think the way a lot of the lone wolves around here do."

The Skid Row lone wolves "wouldn't spit on them old-age homes." Unattached as they have been through most of their lives, and accustomed as they have become to rationalizing their loneliness with talk of freedom, they are not going to be institutionalized now in their old age.

An old Detroiter named Jerry, nicknamed Jerky Jerry, says about institutions: "I rather beg than be put in one of them places where people should tell me everything I should do. I heard them tell a friend of mine: 'Now eat all your food up, young man.' He wasn't no young man either, not unless seventy-three is young nowadays. If you refuse to eat your food, those old-age nurses shove it down your throat. They done it to my friend. Me, I would have spit it back up in their faces. Some old nurse in the home my friend was in hit him with a whip one time. She was a great big awful thing. My friend was a little guy. I'm happy here. I got my pension. Thirteen dollars a week and I live the way I want. Just let everybody leave me alone."

Sixty-nine-year-old Gyppie Johnson is another old man who has adjusted on Skid Row. He moved on to the Bowery in 1949, but he used to come down for week-end benders for many years before he decided to make it his home.

"I used to live in Brooklyn," he says, "with my ma and three of the ugliest old-maid sisters you ever saw. I came down here to get away. All I needed to do when I was home was to get me a little snifter, and Ma'd start in praying God should make her Gyppie a good boy and them four-eyed bastard sisters of mine would stand around telling her she should give me castor oil. Castor oil! I'm sorry I didn't give them castor oil right in their three dopey-looking pusses. I liked coming down here on week ends and drinking all I wanted. I figured out as soon as Ma passed away, not that I ever wished it on her, I was going to kick my sisters in their false plates and come down here to stay. Ma passed away in '49, the year I started drawing my government income, fifty-six dollars a month. I live plenty good on that. My flop is fourteen dollars. I get free grub with the 'soul savers.' If I need a benny in the winter, I take a nose dive, so's they'll give me a coat for free. Any bloody bucket'll let me drink on the cuff. All I got to say is thanks to the government for supporting me good in my old age."

Jerky Jerry and Gyppie Johnson and plenty of other men actually like the Skid Row life. But many old-timers are devastated by it.

Seventy-one-year-old "Mamie" McCree is one who curses the day he first hit the Row. He lives on Vine Street in Philadelphia. He is a slender and effeminate man. His real name is Martin, but the boys on the Row nicknamed him "Mamie." He worked in a laundry in his younger days. He never earned much money and spent all he made on "good living."

"I always liked nice surroundings," he told me. "Curtains on my windows, spreads on my bed, and the kind of a bathroom you wouldn't mind taking a bath in. Now look at me." He hurled his fist against the khaki army blanket covering the single bed in his cubicle in Lowell's flop. "I'd jump out of the window if I had the nerve."

I met old pensioners on the Row who started out hating it as much as "Mamie" McCree did and ended up liking it as much as Gyppie Johnson. And I met many who, although they had rejected the life at the beginning, are adjusted to it now.

"What else," eighty-year-old "Rabbi" Kramer asks, "what else is there? On fifty dollars a month you can go someplace else? A man got to live the best he can. For a man my age is not no more a matter what he likes he should do. For me, is this way, like, schmike, it don't mean a thing. I got to do what I got to do."

5. Blinkies, Halfies, Crazies, Dummies

Skid Row, U.S.A., is a refuge for handicapped people. Blind men, called "blinkies," live here; and men who limp or carry crutches, called "crips"; and "halfies," whose legs are off below the knees; and "wingies" who have no arms; and mentally ill people known as "crazies"; and feeble-minded folk called "dummies." They blend in with the mass in this home of the disinherited and are warmly welcomed into the membership of any group they want to affiliate with. Many of them possess something the vast majority of egoless ones along Skid Row do not have—a fighting spirit. They are hostile people on the whole, full of bitterness and anger.

Many handicapped Rowers live on disability pensions and beg, mostly without much success, when they need extra money for eating, sleeping, and especially for drinking. But some of them have become highly successful beggars. They utilize many chicaneries which are based on psychological and sociological truisms. Outsiders would be amazed at the amount of factual analysis that goes into the small matter of picking out potential pros-

pects, for example. There are handicapped people along Skid Row who collect two hundred dollars to three hundred dollars a week. They can afford to live any place they want to but continue to stay on the Row because the egoless mass down there provides them with constant ego-lifts.

Robert Dean, a crip with both his legs in braces, is very popular along the Bowery. He is considered a wit in some circles and a societal benefactor in others. He is cultivated and catered to, and the fact that he always has money enough for treating people to bottles of sneaky or glasses of beer is only incidentally responsible.

"I am a beggar," he says casually, "and I could have an apartment on Park Avenue if I wanted one. I don't like to live among rich people. They think too much of themselves and look down on people like me. Here, everybody admires me for my brains and personality. My crippled legs aren't important. Get it?"

I got it. I watched Robert Dean, a paunchy, red-faced man in his thirties, operate in the New Yorker on the Bowery. He sat at the head of a large table and summoned people over to drink with him. All the alkies came and drank and outdid each other in telling him what a great man he was.

"My father and mother wish they were dead every time they think of me down on the Bowery," Robert Dean says with infinite satisfaction. "It's embarrassing for them. I can just see the old man straighten up his back—he always carries himself straight as a ramrod anyhow—and try to explain me away. 'As God is my witness, I always did the best for that boy.' Mother'd put her two cents in too. God forbid anybody should think she hadn't done her part by her poor crippled son. She always told about how I was her cross and she would bear me with dignity."

"No wonder you wanted to get away from them," I said.

He said, "You don't know the half of it. Nobody does."

Everybody he knew pitied Robert Dean from the time he was a baby—his aunts and uncles, his neighbors, his brother Dick and two sisters, Jean and Mary Anne.

"Dick was a year younger than I was," he says, "Jean was three years younger, and Mary Anne was four years younger, but they were always sorry for me. My mother and father saw to it. Father once licked Dick because he took his own ball away from me. I felt sorry for Dick until I heard my mother tell him that he was getting old enough to help her share her cross—me, that is—and that God would reward him for being kind. I often thought my mother enjoyed having me crippled."

"Why did you?" I asked.

He said, "Lots of reasons. The way she talked to Dick was one. Honest to God, little as I was, I could tell she had pleasure in her voice. She used to encourage me to get fat as a pig. She filled me full of ice cream and candy. I weighed a hundred and forty pounds when I was ten years old. Mother always insisted on carrying me down the front steps. I didn't need her to. I could get around with the two braces I wore."

I said, "You must have been some load for her."

He smiled. "Yup. She was a little woman, too. She sprained her back carrying me one day. I was glad. I thought, 'Now she'll really have a cross to bear.'"

Robert Dean cannot remember a time when he didn't feel hatred toward everyone in his vicinity. He hunted an outlet from the time he was a little boy.

"I used to walk down around here back when I was eleven years old. I came down around Delancey Street and Rivington Street to watch the people and buy things from the pushcarts. My mother never knew where I went. She didn't even like me walking in my own neighborhood, Seventy-third Street and Riverside Drive, because she said people were cruel and might hurt my feelings. That was a good one. After all the times she'd hurt me, she worried about other people hurting my feelings."

"Did they?" I asked. "As much down here as in your neighborhood?"

"Sure," he said. "Only it never hurt so much. For some reason."

"Maybe it was because you didn't consider them your equals," I said.

He said, "Maybe."

"Did you make any friends?" I asked.

He said, "I made a sort of a friend when I was four-teen."

I said, "Would you tell me about him, Robert?"

He said, "There isn't much to tell."

I said, "What was his name?"

He said, "Billy O'Callaghan."

I said, "How old was Billy?"

He said, "Sixteen. He was almost six feet tall. He had curly hair and blue eyes and nice, straight, white teeth. He smiled a lot."

I said, "How did you come to meet him?"

"He started talking to me in a cafeteria I went to once in a while," Robert said. "He sat down at my table and said, 'Hi,' and started asking me a lot of personal questions about why I was there. He wanted to know how much money my family had, and what did a drip like me do with his braces when he had a girl?"

I said, "Didn't you mind his questions?"

"No," he said, "I never minded anything Billy did."

I said, "I take it you knew him a long time."

He said, "Yes. Professionally. He and I began working together. I was his stool."

I said, "What was that?"

He said, "Assistant, I guess you'd call it. We formed a sweet little racket. I used to sit on a corner curbstone on a busy street and look miserable. When prosperous-looking people went by I'd stop them and ask them for money. I didn't use any particular line, since that was Billy's business. If they gave me something, fine. If they didn't, Billy'd come out from behind the corner he was watching from and give out with the line. He was really good."

"What did he say?" I asked.

"Always different things, depending on the look of the people he was trying to make," Robert said. "He usually talked about what a pitiful cripple I was and said that my father would murder me if I didn't bring a certain amount of money home that night."

"How did you divide the proceeds?" I asked.

"Half and half," he said.

"How long did you and Billy continue your racket?" I asked.

"About three years," he said, "till Billy got sent up the river for a burglary job he pulled."

"You must have missed him," I said.

He said, "Like crazy. He did a lot for me. He used to talk to me like a big brother. He told me I was a stupid fool for being ashamed of my legs since I didn't have anything to do with making them, and that I should use being a cripple to make a place for myself in the world."

I said, "The way you used it when you begged?"

He said, "That and other ways. He said I could use it with girls."

"Was he right?" I asked.

"He seemed to be," he said. "The first girl I tried it with came right to me."

The girl's name was Eloise Watson, and she was fifteen years old when Robert Dean was seventeen. She was a member of Billy's crowd. She was no beauty—Billy considered her homely—but Robert thought she was very pretty. She had red hair, green eyes, and very fair skin. She had had a crush on Billy ever since Robert had met her, and she always made it plain. But Billy was cool toward her.

One day Robert discussed Eloise with Billy. "I love her so much," he said, "I get a pain inside whenever I look at her."

Billy laughed.

Robert said, "I mean it."

Billy went on laughing.

Robert said, "I think I'm going to quit coming down here, Billy."

Billy said, "You can't do that."

Robert said, "I got to do it. I get sick when I look at Eloise. I can't sleep a couple of nights after I've seen her."

"Why can't you sleep?" Billy asked.

He was ashamed to admit why, but he did anyhow. "I want her so bad I get a pain runs right up inside of me."

"Only one thing to do about that," Billy said.

Robert became angry. "That's O.K. for you, big shot. But I'm not you. Why should a girl have anything to do with me? Eloise doesn't want a cripple when there are plenty of healthy fellows with two good legs around."

Billy said, "That's just it."

"What's just it?"

"What you said before, dope. Plenty of healthy fellows around but no cripples she can feel sorry over and think she's doing them a big favor."

Robert said, "Billy, you're crazy." But he wasn't so sure. Why couldn't his crippled legs be his weapons with Eloise? They always had gotten him what he wanted. His little racket and Billy's for example—what would all of

Billy's eloquence avail him without Robert's legs stretched out on the curb?

Billy called Eloise and asked her whether he and Robert could come over one Saturday night. She said she'd be glad to have them come. He asked whether her folks would be out, and she giggled coyly and said they would.

Robert felt strained and uncomfortable, but he tried to act sophisticated. "Always the contact man, hunh Billy?" he said.

Billy laughed and said he'd never known a little contact to do anybody any harm yet.

Eloise lived in a railroad flat on Avenue A. There was a dirty kitchen and two filthy bedrooms. Standing in the kitchen and looking in at the two unmade beds in the first bedroom, Robert says today that he suddenly wished, for the first time in his life, that he were in his mother's excruciatingly well-ordered home.

Eloise said, "Sit down, fellows," indicating two rickety kitchen chairs that showed signs of having been painted white once.

Before Robert could sit, Billy jumped to his side and put a hefty hand on his arm. "Let me help you, kid," he said. He turned to Eloise. "The poor guy's been suffering all day. His legs've been paining him something terrible. Not that he ever complained about them or nothing. Robert just ain't a complaining kid. But his face showed me how bad he was feeling."

Robert obligingly gave a version of the suffering face.

"Please don't talk like that," he said. "My troubles are my own business."

Billy looked upset. "Robert Dean, you should be ashamed. You ain't giving Eloise credit for nothing. She got the kindest heart of any girl around here. She wants to know your troubles and help you out. Right, honey?"

Eloise nodded.

Robert said, "A poor cripple like me has no right to take up her time."

Billy said, "But she wants to help you. That's the kind of kid Eloise is. Ain't it?"

Eloise said, "Yeah, Billy, sure."

Billy stayed about an hour, and by the time he said good-by Eloise was as ready as Robert to have him go.

"I guess I learned from Eloise what I could get people to do because I was a cripple. She wanted me worse than I did her that first night, just couldn't wait to get her clothes off and started grabbing at mine. She turned out to be a real pushover. But that wasn't the point. I got good girls with the same line I used on Eloise. One kid named Maria was a virgin before I got her. She wouldn't give out to any of the fellows, not even Billy himself."

Robert Dean moved onto the Bowery when he was twenty-one. He moved into a room at the Blue Bird flop.

"It wasn't really a room," he says. "It was a cubicle. Incidentally, I should not say was. I still live there." He smiled. "It's really such a terrible place, I can't help but wish they admitted women."

I said, "You wouldn't want to bring your girls to the Blue Bird, Robert."

"Not my girls," he said, "my mother. I'd like to see her face."

Robert Dean will doubtless never leave the Bowery, or, if he does go anywhere, it will be no farther than the Skid Row of some other city.

"Don't tell me I'm crazy," he says, "but I feel more at home in the Blue Bird and greasies and buckets than I ever felt uptown."

Mackie Chambers is another handicapped beggar who lives on Skid Row because he prefers to. He is an amputee who has stubs where his legs should be. He earns anywhere from $150 to $350 a week. He and his wife Louisa and his daughter Lady occupy a three-room cold-water flat on First Street near the Bowery, for which they pay $22 a month.

"Where else am I going to live?" he asks. "Sure, I could pay $122 a month . . . $222 . . . $322. I ain't the only one in my family working. Louisa works too. Of course, she's such a big, fat dummy, she don't make out so good. But my daughter, Lady, can make near as much as me when she puts her mind to it. We could live anyplace we wanted, but I like living with my own people. In this neighborhood people like to listen to you. They don't make you shut up before you get started good on your stories."

Mackie Chambers's stories depend on his moods. The story of how he came to be a halfie is subject to several interpretations. He cries over himself during his maudlin periods. His watery blue eyes turn red and his pasty white bullet face goes baby pink. But during his happy times he claps himself on the back and tells his story with the air of a devil-may-care sportsman who can laugh at his misfortunes.

"My old man had plenty of moolah. A millionaire. A big shot. He liked to tell people what to do, direct them around, you do this, you do that. I used to answer him back. I'd say, 'Don't tell me what to do.' He kicked me out of his house."

Mackie said he had no way of supporting himself after his father kicked him out.

"Only thing I was good for was to be a rich man's son. I could sing beautiful, tra la la, and play the piano. Nobody wanted to pay me for singing, so I got a job as foreman on a construction deal. That's how come I'm all crippled up."

A large iron beam was supposed to have fallen on him and to have crushed both his legs.

"The doctor was sorry for me. But I ain't the kind of guy to go around feeling sorry for myself. Not Mackie Chambers. I told the doctor, 'Listen, butcher, you done the best you can, so that's all I can expect. You been a straight guy with me, and I ain't blaming you for nothing. Stop worrying about my feet. Take a lesson from me. The only worry I got about these stubs, they keep my head so close to the ground, I'm only afraid I'm gonna get tuber-cu-lo-sis!'"

"I used to have two good feet, the same as the next guy," he tells during his bitter periods. "But I wasn't satisfied to be healthy. I had to be a patriotic American and enlist in the 1914 World War. Nobody told me to do it. I went and done it on my own. I got shot in the feet right before the Armistice was signed. The big shots in Europe were happy about the Armistice. 'It's peace. Hurray! Hurray!' But they never took me or the other crippled soldiers home from Germany. They left us in Berlin to rot. There was no way to make a living there, so we had to go out begging. That's what America done for me."

Mrs. Louisa Chambers swears she married Mackie before any World War I was contemplated and that he was a cripple then.

"When Mr. Chambers"—she always refers to him as Mr. Chambers—"and me got married up, he was a poor, pitiful cripple the same like he is today. Only there was more money in them good old days. People had hearts made them give to such a pitiful cripple. He did better when he was a young man. But he was meaner too. I was more scared of him then."

Not that she isn't still scared of him. Her "poor, pitiful cripple" of a husband has only to lift an eyebrow at her and she is reduced to helpless tears.

"He beats me up all the time," she says. "He tells me, 'Go on, get down on the floor, Louisa. Stretch yourself out.' Then he takes a broom and he beats me up. He says he only does it because I'm fat."

Louisa Chambers has worked as a "house-beggar" through most of her married life. She rings doorbells and asks housewives to give her money.

"I never made the kind of money Mr. Chambers made, though," she says. "He's a pretty lucky fellow. All he needs to do is ride around the streets in his cart and show his stumps out. Once in a while he uses a smart trick he does with dry bread. When some rich lady all dressed up in a fur coat comes by him, he takes this dry, old bread he carries around and throws it on the sidewalk. When she gets real close to him he grabs it up and starts in chewing it. I never had no sweet thing like that to count on. For a while I had Lady, though. I used to bring her with me when I went begging. She was such a skinny thing I'd show her to people and say, 'I think my Lady's going to die, because I can't afford to feed her good.' But then, before we got her trained in right, Mr. Chambers said it wasn't no life for his kid and I got to stop carrying her with me."

Today Mr. Chambers is not very fond of his daughter Lady, because she is not as respectful to him as he thinks a daughter should be; but he once loved her very much.

"I went and moved out of this neighborhood to make things nice for Lady," he says. "I came up to Sixtieth Street where the swells live. Lady was eight years old. I had a tough time getting the apartment I wanted. A superintendent or something asked me all kinds of questions —what did I do and where did I work? I told him I was a millionaire."

The Chambers family lived on Sixtieth Street for three years. None of them was very happy there—not even Lady. The other children snubbed her, because her father was a cripple and her mother was not as smart as their mothers were. She never made a friend on Sixtieth Street. When she was eleven she begged her father to return to Avenue B.

"I was glad when Lady told me herself she wanted to go back where we came from. I like living around my kind of people."

They moved into the tenement they still occupy today. Lady was very happy on Avenue B until she was about fifteen and her baby brother, Robert, was born.

"My father was crazy about Bobby," she said. "I wasn't jealous. I loved him myself. But my old man started hating me the minute Bobby was born, and he began hating me more and more as Bobby grew older. He said awful things to me. I began to hate being home. He used to yell at my mother: 'A big girl like her laying around the house and going to school while I got to drag my crippled body around to give her eat and drink. Why don't she go out and do something for herself?' I didn't know what I could do since I hadn't finished high school, but he said there was no law about my having to finish. So I started truanting from school and begging on my own."

Now she is thirty-one and still begs for a living. She is a slender, pretty woman with limpid brown eyes and long brown hair worn in a loose bun.

"If a sucker wants to give," she says, "why shouldn't I be the one to benefit? I give him something he needs in return for the money—the feeling that he's a pretty great guy."

Although she is not physically handicapped herself, Lady has absorbed the handicapped beggars' philosophy. She pretends to be handicapped when she begs. She throws her hip joint out of place in such a way as to convince everyone who sees her that she lives with constant pain.

I once accompanied Lady Chambers on a begging trip. We boarded the Fifth Avenue downtown bus at Seventy-sixth Street. Or rather, I boarded it. Lady tried to. Her bad hip prevented her. Try as she would, she just could not make that first step. The tension on her pretty face, wetting now with perspiration engendered by the almost superhuman effort she'd made to help herself, showed how hard she was trying.

The bus driver left his seat. He came down to where Lady was standing. "Let me help you, ma'am," he said. He lifted her onto the bus and into a seat.

Lady thanked him with exactly the proper degree of pride. She is a woman who respects the small nuance. Her smile, her hand gesture, her every move were so expressive they cried to be noticed.

"I wish I didn't have to trouble you, sir."

"Oh ma'am." The bus driver was the picture of old-time chivalry. "No trouble at all."

Two of the women sitting on either side of Lady smiled at her. They had come every inch of the way with her. She smiled back, shyly but appreciatively. Then she remembered something. Oh dear, she told the conductor, in all that awful fuss and flurry she had forgotten to pay her fare. What a dreadful thing. She opened her purse and began rummaging around for her change purse. A look of panic settled on her face.

"Conductor. I don't know where——" She looked inside her purse once more. "It's just—I seem to have lost my money."

"Don't worry about that, ma'am," the conductor said.

"But my fare——"

"Aw, skip the fare."

"I couldn't do that. I'll return it, of course. Tomorrow, I'll——" She grew suddenly hesitant. "No, I guess I can't return it tomorrow, after all." She turned toward the well-dressed, elderly woman sitting to the right of her. "I get a pension check every two weeks, and I just got one yesterday and—well——" She ran a small hand over her smooth head.

"Can you stop payment, my dear?" the woman asked.

"It's too late. I cashed it as soon as I got it. I have to cash my checks right away. I have to live on them."

The woman said, "Oh."

Lady rubbed her hands together. She wet her lips with her tongue. "I never bothered strangers with my problems before. Excuse me."

"What will you do?" the woman asked. "How are you going to live?"

"Well, I have a brother——" Then, in a lower voice, almost in a whisper as though talking to herself, "No, that's out, I guess."

"What's out?" the woman asked.

"Getting a few dollars from my brother. Most times I

could borrow from him—but just now—his little boy was taken to the hospital yesterday, and he needs every penny he can get his hands on. I don't know what's the matter with me, talking out my troubles to somebody I never met before. But there's something about you. You're easy to talk to. Please don't let me bother you though."

"Bother?" the woman grabbed Lady's arm. "You aren't bothering me. I was just wondering—would you accept a small loan?"

"No, I couldn't really——" Lady withdrew her arm. "It's so nice of you, but we don't know each other and——"

The old woman said, "Please. You can return it when you're able——"

"I couldn't. Really."

"Of course you could. Make believe you know me. As a matter of fact, I hope we will be getting to know each other."

Lady hoped so, too. The old woman was the kindest person she'd ever met. All the same, she just couldn't take money from her.

Finally the old woman managed to induce Lady to accept a small ten-dollar loan. They exchanged addresses, and Lady said she would be sure to pay the money back.

"I could have gotten more than ten dollars from her, if I'd wanted to go to the trouble of playing her right," Lady told me later.

I said, "Didn't you feel a little bit sorry for her?"

Lady said, "Why should I have?"

I said, "Because she was old and probably not very rich. She may miss that ten dollars, for all you know."

"Let her miss it," Lady said. "She'll tell her friends a story about me that'll be worth a whole lot more than ten dollars to her. I don't feel sorry for suckers. I laugh at them."

Lady has absorbed her "sucker" theory from her crippled father and feeble-minded mother. She knows it too.

"The old man wouldn't be happy if he didn't beg," she says. "The money he makes is the least of what he gets out of it. Outsmarting the suckers is the important thing. He can think to himself, 'I'm a lot brainier than those other people, even if they do have two good legs.'"

I met many handicapped beggars who illustrated Lady's point. The money they make is secondary to the pleasure of the chase, and the amount of the money is important primarily because it proves the chase to have been worth while. When they get together, either formally or informally, they brag about their begging proceeds and then compare their personal tricks and discuss them theoretically with a view to helping one another. They did that all evening at a party Mackie Chambers invited me to.

The party was held one Saturday night in Mackie's four-room flat on Avenue B. When I arrived, I found that Louisa had painted her small living room for the occasion. Three walls were a sort of plum purple and the fourth was pea green. The fresh paint extended about halfway up the wall, since, as Louisa explained to all new guests, she was too fat to reach very high. A huge picture of Mackie Chambers smiling out of his cart adorned the green wall. Ivy plants, the fruits of Louisa's labor, grew in wild profusion all over the small room. There was one easy chair, and there were two or three wooden ones.

By the time I arrived, a few of the guests had been forced to take seats on the red-and-green-striped straw rug and were taking long drinks out of an unlabeled quart bottle.

Mackie Chambers asked Louisa to introduce me to his guests. They were Si Greener and his wife Rita, both crutch crips; a blinky named Bill Blandon, whom everyone called Blindey; a young fellow about twenty-two with saliva dropping down from his mouth who was introduced as "Cuckoo"; and the young fellow's current girl, Beatrice, who had two shrunken arms and a humped back.

"My father was glad when I was born like this," she told me, in what seemed to be a crack aimed at Lady Chambers, "because then when I went begging I was just the most genu-wine thing."

In addition to Lady there were three other uncrippled guests: an old-timer with a gray, shoulder-length, page-boy haircut pushed back from a high forehead and sparkling black eyes in a leathery face, a plain woman of twenty-seven or thereabouts who wore horn-rimmed glasses, and a man in his early thirties, tall, broadly built, with curly black hair he kept running his hands through. The old-timer's name was Laronian, and he said he wrote poetry as a hobby. The plain girl and curly-haired man were husband and wife. They were Mel and Mame Roberts. Both of them were narcotics addicts.

By the time I arrived, the party was off to a roaring professional discussion of tricks of the trade.

"I got five bucks from a old gent yesterday easy as pie," Beatrice, the humpbacked girl, said.

"What did you do?" Lady asked. "Tell him he could touch your hump for luck?"

"Nope," Beatrice said. "My hump never came into it. I just told him he looked young enough to be fighting in Korea."

"How old did he look?" Lady asked.

Beatrice said, "Sixty, sixty-two."

"And he went for your line?" Lady said.

Beatrice said, "Sure did. I went up to him and said, 'Excuse me, mister, but I've got a brother fighting in Korea, and I'm wondering if you could've maybe run into him while you was over there yourself. I can tell from looking at you that you must have been in the Air Force.' He laughed and said he was too old to fight. So I stepped back a little bit and I looked like I thought somebody was off their nut, him or me or somebody. 'Too old?' I said. 'You mean *you* are too old? How do they want them these days, out of the cradle?'"

Everybody laughed at Beatrice.

"Old men are pretty good deals," Lady said.

Mr. Chambers said, "Old ladies are better."

Mel Roberts said, "Fairy boys are best."

"Yeah," his wife Mame said. "For you, doll."

Mel ignored his wife's interruption. "I scoff all the fairy joints in the Village." He turned to me. "Greenwich Village. Those guys are the easiest touches in the world."

"Easy touches, hell," Mame said. "They look at you and figure you'd be good in bed. They ain't giving you nothing for free but paying for services they hope to get."

"They never got nothing from me yet," Mel said, "and you know it."

"How do I know it?" Mame asked in a soft, impersonal voice.

Mel said, "Because I tell you, that's how."

The white-haired poet Laronian smiled gently. "Please, no fights," he said.

Mame said, "Who's fighting?"

"Yeah, who?" Mel said.

Laronian said, "Mame, you got no right to be so suspicious about fairy boys. They're awful good. They're like whores and niggers." He turned to me. "All the old beggars know that fairy boys and whores and niggers gives good, better than rich people."

I said, "Why is that?"

"Well," Laronian said, "they feel like we and they are brothers under the skin. People who don't like us aren't crazy about them either. Then, too, they feel important when they give. Rich people feel important without having to give anything to beggars."

Such is the logic of the Skid Row beggars I met. They are psychologists by instinct. They are not educated or particularly intelligent or sensitive, judged by usual stand-

123

ards, and yet they know that homosexuals are good prospects for them, not alone because they may have sexual designs, but also because they are isolated, unhappy people themselves and would feel empathic to other sufferers. They consider prostitutes the second best givers and Negroes the third best for the same reasons.

"The blacker the niggers, the better they give," the poet Laronian said. "They get mean when they get to be those off-white colors."

Homely little Cuckoo backed him up. "The blackest niggers got the kindest hearts," he said, "and the coal-black ones is the best little givers you want to meet."

Cuckoo and Laronian know somehow that Negroes have been made color-conscious, just as white people are, and that darker Negroes are more likely to need the ego satisfaction of being able to give to people who are worse off than they are. Still in line with accepted psychiatric and sociological theories, beggars rate foreigners immediately below Negroes as potential givers.

Beggars' folklore divides people according to their religion. Catholics are the most generous givers and far more popular with the begging fraternity than Protestants and Jews are.

"Catholic priests are the kindest men in the world," the poet Laronian says. "Nuns are the kindest ladies. Jews and Protestants stink, but Protestants stink worse, especially ministers. A Jew will tell you right off the bat he don't want to give you nothing, but Protestant ministers'll use up all your time asking you questions. After you get done answering them, all they got to offer you's a god-damn job."

Beggars' lore divides potential givers according to age, sex, and physical type. It says that grandmothers, young girls, and married women of thirty are very generous, that single women of forty are a miserly lot on the whole, and that fat women give more readily than slim ones do.

"Fat women are sentimental," Laronian the poet explains. "They are also lazier than skinny ones, and they have more time to spend listening to beggars' stories. Besides they love to cry. Tell a fat woman a story that will make her cry, and you'll be in. I just love fat women."

Beggars' lore is concerned with places as well as people. Professionals regard New York, Chicago, and Philadelphia as so-so towns that cannot be mentioned in the same breath with either Jersey City, which is the best begging town in the country, or Boston, which is the worst one.

"Yeah," Mackie Chambers once said, "I ought to do all my scoffing in Jersey City. I'd get to be a millionaire overnight."

His daughter Lady said, "Jersey City'd be too easy for you, Pa." She turned to me. "He likes the challenge in New York. Right, Pa?"

"What do you mean, challenge?" Mackie asked.

Lady said, "You like the job to be hard. You don't want to do anything easy."

"No begging's hard for me," Mackie said. "I ride down any street in the world and people got to give to me. They take one look, and they'd be ashamed to turn me down."

"He's right, you know," Lady said. "Pa's always felt so right about what he was doing that he was able to get money out of people who had stones where their hearts should have been."

Mackie nodded and attempted to look modest.

Mackie Chambers is a clear example of the aggressiveness with which certain handicapped beggars approach their potential beneficiaries. He may whine his thanks to people who give to him, for the maintenance of good will is important in his business. One never knows when or where one may run into people a second time. But actually he feels that he is merely getting what is due him.

Any analysis of handicapped people along Skid Row, U.S.A., must make several separations between types of handicapped people. First, the cripples must be separated from the blind ones. Then separation must be attempted between the crippled minority, the Mackie Chamberses and the Robert Deans who have used their handicaps to become successful beggars, and the majority who live on inadequate pensions and only beg when they need to. It is the same way among the blind. For every successful blind beggar you meet on Skid Row, you also come across numerous men and women who live on pensions of sixty to seventy-five dollars a month and beg, without finesse, when they find they must. Many of them hate Skid Row, but they live here because sixty or seventy-five dollars a month can buy more for a man with a regular income.

Crippy Smith is one like that. He is a great big man whose right leg is shorter than his left and who has no hands. He is forty-one years old and has been living in the New Yorker flop on Chicago's Madison Street since his mother died fifteen years ago.

"I came here when I was twenty-six," he says, "because nobody wanted to have me around. I got one brother in the chicken business and two sisters. They chip in to send me fifty dollars a month, so I'll never come home and bother them. All of them's ashamed of me. Not that I blame them. They're whole people. I should be dead. I wish I was. I'm very weak, and sometimes I get hot flashes hurt me so much I think they'll kill me. But they never do. Cripples like me don't die young. They live long lives. I hate Madison Street so much, but there's no place else for me to go on fifty dollars a month. Some months I can't live on my check. So I stop people I see in the street and ask them to please give me a little money to save me from dying. I ask for a nickel or a couple of pennies."

"What kind of people do you stop?" I asked, thinking of Mackie's elaborate begging theories.

"Anybody comes by," he said simply.

Blinky Langston has no begging theories either. A man of sixty-four, he lives on the Bowery on a seventy-five-dollar-per-month blind man's pension, which he augments with occasional begging.

"I only beg when I got to," he says. "I feel like an animal at a side show. Maybe I shouldn't. I'm only doing what I have to. I can't live on seventy-five dollars a month. Not today. I can't go out and earn money either. I would if I could. So I beg till I make enough to buy the things I need.

Then I stop. Plenty of the other blinkies around here laugh at me and think I'm crazy not to beg more. But I can't help it. I get this awful feeling in me. My friends say I shouldn't. They say, 'What the hell, you're blind, the government ought to be taking care of you better. You ain't to blame because you got to beg. The government is.'"

I said, "Which of your friends say that, Blinky?"

He said, "Most of them. Tucker Granger especially."

I said, "Who's Tucker Granger?"

He said, "He's rich."

Tucker Granger is a Bowery blinky who earns between twenty and twenty-five dollars an hour scoffing mid-Manhattan. He has none of the reservations that Blinky Langston does.

"What do you think I am, a crazy as well as a blinky?" he said, when I asked whether he minded begging for a living. "Why should I mind? You know what I'd be doing if I didn't beg, don't you? Living like all the rest of them on a government pension. I been begging since I was ten years old, and I'm sixty-one now."

Most of the more successful blind beggars are about Tucker's age. They grew up before 1935 when blind aid was first made available. Many of them were raised to be beggars, because there was no other practicable way for blind children from poor families to exist. They never learned to think in terms of pensions or sheltered workshops, and so it is natural that they would not think in those terms today. They laugh when you try to discuss blind-aid projects with them. You can't really blame them for laughing, once you see the picture from where they sit.

Take the matter of blind pensions. No state pays its blind more than $80 a month. Some states pay a $50 maximum. In 1951, the total expenditure of the entire country for blind pensions came to $4,668,119 for 97,-129 people. It averaged $40 per person. A good blind beggar can make $40 a day if he wants to.

"For all I care," Tucker Granger says, "they can take their pensions and stick them. Yours truly will go right on begging for a living, thank you very much."

Tucker Granger was raised to be a beggar.

"My father worked in a dress shop," he says. "He used to make about fourteen dollars a week when he worked. He worked about seven months out of twelve. There were five children besides me. My mother and father talked about me at night when they thought I was sleeping and couldn't hear them. My father told my mother she better face facts. I'd have to go begging when I got big. What else could a blind boy do? My mother'd say, yeah, but why wasn't there a school where I could get educated and learn to do something could make me a living? My father'd say, 'Why? People like us don't know why. All we can do is the best we can. Tucker's got to learn to beg, so when we die he can help himself.'"

"How old were you when you started begging?" I said.

He said, "Ten, like I told you before. I wasn't kidding, you know!"

I said, "How did you feel?"

He said, "The way any boy feels when he starts in a new job."

I said, "You mean you felt scared?"

He said, "A little."

I said, "Were you ashamed?"

He said, "No. What of? It's no disgrace to keep yourself alive, is it? I'd feel more ashamed if I had to work at one of the crummy jobs they give blind people."

Certainly the jobs that are available to blind people are routine and low-paying on the whole—caning chairs, making brooms. This is the case even in cities having the most effective workshop programs, New York and its highly respected New York Workshop for the Blind, for instance.

Interestingly, under the circumstances, Stanley Wartenburg, blind director of employment for the Workshop, recently deplored the practice of giving to blind beggars.

"This is a wonderfully rich city, full of kind people who are touched by panhandlers, some of whom come from Pennsylvania and New Jersey to work the streets and then go home to rest up for a while," he said. "It is a concept of blindness that we don't like. We know that if these people were really interested in going to work, they could get jobs. Investigations have shown that some of them are collecting, not making, $168 a week."

What jobs could these people do to earn as much money as they make begging, though? Few, if any. Mr. Wartenburg's own agency employs 37 blind people on its staff, a few, like Mr. Wartenburg, in high administrative positions. One hundred and thirty-eight blind people work at the agency's industrial plant; 209 have been placed in charge of newsstands and concessions. There are 78 blind people in New York exceptional enough to work as dictaphone operators with private industrial companies; 40 are practicing in the professions; 37 own their own businesses and 27 are salesmen. The rest cane chairs and do other routine jobs. Few of the blind people associated with the Workshop earn anywhere near $168 a week. Many handicapped people who don't beg wish they did—or could. They are angry at themselves because, the way they figure it, they have "a good thing" in their handicap and don't know how to use it. They think they are hopelessly stupid and the only Rowers they consider lower than themselves are the dopies and the crazies.

Dopies and crazies are all over Skid Row, U.S.A. You don't have to be a psychiatrist to spot them. It is an even chance that, wherever you happen to find yourself, you'll see many of them, men and women who wear their psychoses right out on their sleeves. They wander about uncared for and often hungry. They are unable to support themselves and, even when help is offered, many of them are prevented by their delusions from accepting it. You often see them with the look of starvation bright on their faces. Volunteer to buy them a meal, and watch them scurry away, smiling, frightened of having offended you, but knowing all the same that they'd rather eat dirt than the food you wish to give them.

Irving Kane is an old-timer along the Bowery. Pig Head

Hattie introduced me to him. He is only thirty-seven years old, a big man with hardly any flesh on his bones.

"This is Irv," Pig Head told me. "He's hungry."

As a rule I don't take Pig Head seriously when she tells me her friends are hungry. Whenever they meet me, they're either hungry or thirsty. Irving Kane was different though. That starved look was all over him. I said, "Please come and eat some lunch with me."

He shook his head no.

Pig Head said, "Aw, come off it, Irv. This girl'll buy anything you want to eat. Besides, she's no long-haired preacher'll tell you what's wrong. Her meals are for free." She turned to me. "Poor fellow's crazier than a bedbug, you know."

I said, "Please eat lunch with me."

Irving Kane went on shaking his head no. But he did permit Pig Head and me to lead him to the Canary Cafeteria on Delancey Street. It took about three minutes before we could get him to come in. Then we had a time getting him seated. Pig Head sat with him while I bought his lunch, a bacon and tomato sandwich, milk, and deep-dish apple pie. I set it down. I said, "I hope you enjoy it, Irv."

He smiled weakly. "I can't eat it," he said. Then he stopped smiling and stood up and shook his hand in my face. "It's poison," he shouted. He kicked at the table and ran out of the door.

Then there is Aldous Johnson of Philadelphia. He flops around Vine Street in vacant doorways when he can find them and right out in the street when he can't. He is fifty-four years old with a kindly face and long hair, which he pulls to make himself scream. He says he authored *Alice in Wonderland,* the *Collected Works of Charles Dickens,* and the *Encyclopaedia Britannica.*

"There are some who think I wrote the Bible," he says. "I did not write the Bible. Those who accuse me of having done so are liars. I will be avenged upon them."

Aldous is a familiar figure around Philadelphia's Skid Row. Occasionally, some kind Rower will attempt to care for him but the kindness seldom lasts long, for Aldous gets to feeling mean sometimes and lashing out at people.

"I tried to help old Aldous out a couple times," an old Philadelphia Rower named Ralphie Sylvester said. "I brung him sandwiches to an alley he was flopping in one night. He ate them all up, then started getting ready to punch me in the nose. I didn't want to tangle with him, so I ran away. I found a cop a couple of blocks from Aldous's alley and tried to tell him about Aldous. He wouldn't listen. He told me, 'All you bums can make up the best stories.' I said, 'I'm not asking you to take my word. Walk over to that alley with me. It's not far. You'll see him with your own eyes. I tell you what, if I'm telling you a lie, you can arrest me.' He still didn't want to go, but I told him if that crazy man died in his alley he'd be to blame. He got mad then. He said, 'All right, bum, but if this is another story, I feel sorry for you.' I said, 'If it's a story, you can do anything you want to me. O.K.?' He said, 'Yeah,' and we began walking. What do you think happened when we got to old Aldous's alley?"

I said, "He wasn't there. He'd walked away while you were gone."

"You're wrong," he said, "Dumb loony did worse than walk away. He seen the copper and stood up very respectable like. He said, 'How do you do, officer?' The copper says, 'How are you feeling?' Aldous says, 'Very fine, your honor, thank you very much. And how are you, sir?' I tell you, the cop was mad as hell. He gave me a look and then he says, 'Yeah, sure, somebody standing in this alley is crazy all right, but it ain't this man here,' he points his finger at Aldous, 'and it ain't me,' meaning himself, 'but it sure is somebody else in this alley.' I guess you know what he meant by that, huh?"

I said, "I guess I do."

He said, "He told Aldous good-by very polite, and then he gave me a little knock with his stick. He says, 'You're a lucky bum. I could pull you in for trying to mislead an officer. I'll let you off now. But if there's ever a next time——' So after he was gone, I speak to Aldous like he's a person instead of a crazy. I say, 'Aldous, I was only trying to do you a favor because I'm your friend. I didn't want to get you arrested. I figured out no judge would keep you in jail long but send you to a nice clean booby hatch so's you won't have to sleep in alleys no more.' No insult about that, is there? Still and all, Aldous swung out and hit me so hard I fell down on the ground. He kept on hitting me till I thought I'd get killed. I asked him to please let me up but he didn't hear me, because he was too busy talking to his voices."

I said, "What voices?"

He said, "Oh, all kinds. That's the trouble with these crazies around here. When you try doing something for them, you mustn't forget their voices. I used to forget till Aldous beat me up. No more."

Skid Rowers are highly tolerant of the mentally handicapped. They shun only those with whom they have negative experiences of the kind that Ralphie Sylvester had with Aldous. The harmless ones go unmolested, and kinder Rowers sometimes even help them maintain their delusions. The only crazies who have anything to fear along Skid Row, U.S.A., are the few who have material possessions on them. Many men along the Row would do anything for money to buy sneaky with, and you sometimes see crazies with mangled limbs and bloodied heads and minus their overcoats, shoes, and suits.

But the crazies are not hurt by other Rowers nearly as often as the dopies are—particularly those who have enough zest to beg for a living and may be expected to have occasional change on them. You meet beaten-up dopies around the hospital emergency wards of every city in this country.

I met Jimmy Nelson of the Bowery in New York's Bellevue Hospital Emergency Ward. He was about nineteen years old, blond-haired, blue-eyed, delicate-featured. He would have been handsome, if his blue eyes hadn't looked so blank. He had come to Bellevue Emergency with a split head but was unable to explain how he had gotten it or what had happened to him. He mistook me for a person in authority at Bellevue.

"I want to milk cows," he said, the first time I talked with him. The second time he said, "I want to go where little children are." After I grew to know him well he asked me to buy his suit for fifteen cents.

I said, "Jimmy, you couldn't sell me your suit. It's the only one you've got. If you sold it to me you'd have nothing to wear, would you?"

He smiled happily. "No," he said, "I'd be naked."

I said, "You must need fifteen cents badly. What will you do with it if I give it to you?"

He smiled again. "Put it in my pocket."

Then there is John Beetle. He is forty-three years old, a puny runt with a huge mouth and a nose that must have been straight and long before some pugilist remodeled it for him. Beetle begs for a living in Chicago.

"Where do you beg?" I asked him.

"Around."

"Around where?"

"Where it's busy."

"How much money do you make?"

"Money."

"How much money?"

"Money. Money."

John Beetle lives like Jimmy Nelson, from hand to mouth. Some nights he sleeps in flops. Other nights he "carries the banner." Whether he flops in a bed or "carries the banner" depends in the first place on what his begging proceeds have been and in the second on what pals he has happened to fall in with. I've known Johnny Beetle to "carry the banner" after earning six dollars or seven dollars, because his good pals, picked up in some saloon that very night, needed money for flopping, eating, buying sneaky pete, and going to see prostitutes.

"I like to give my friends money," he would say on such a night. "I'd rather do that than flop in a bed."

So long as he is able to beg and give his money away, he is comparatively happy. He has no thought for his future.

"Johnny," I once said, "what'll happen when you get too weak to beg for money?"

"I'll lay down and sleep," he said.

I said, "Where?"

He said, "Anyplace."

I said, "In a room?"

He said, "Yeah."

I said, "But you need money to pay for a room. If you're too weak to beg, you won't have any money. Then you won't be able to pay for a room."

He said, "No."

I said, "What'll you do then?"

"'Carry the banner,'" he said simply.

"And if it's cold?" I asked.

He shrugged.

I said, "You wouldn't like being out in cold weather every single night. Would you, Johnny?"

He said, "No."

I said, "Give some of the money you make now to Mr. Burden." Mr. Burden is the manager of the Blue Star, a flop Johnny likes to use when he has money.

He said, "Then I couldn't treat my friends."

I said, "Treat yourself good first and worry about your friends later. Everybody else does."

He smiled at me. "Now why should I go and do that?" he asked.

6. Love on the Row

Skid Row, U.S.A., is tolerant in matters of love as in every other phase of living. Sex takes on diverse forms, and there is no recognized norm. Most alliances are temporary. If there is a man who is regarded as deviant here, it is the rare one who undertakes marriage.

A few of the younger Rowers manage, despite themselves, to "shack up" with good women who are in love with them. But most do not approve these relationships. They are incapable of returning love and contemptuous of the women who stoop to have anything to do with them. The harder the women try to win their love, the more able they become to negate the women. Actually, most of them prefer alliances with women who are transient and easy of affection. Those who have the contact and can afford the tariff seek burlesque girls out. Working Rowers with seasonal jobs have been known to spend a whole summer's "roll" on a few lush weeks with a "burleycue gal." But burlesque girls are for the lucky few. Those who can't get them sometimes try to make do with *prostitutes. Rowers know only two kinds of prostitutes—* "live ones," *who are younger and cleaner than the majority and* "fleabags," *old-timers in their sixties and even seventies who came onto Skid Row because they could not meet the competition elsewhere. They are very dirty, and most of them are known to be syphilitics. Many men who can't abide* "fleabags" *and are unable to get* "live ones" *form transient homosexual attachments that last for a few weeks or months or even years and then break up without anybody's getting hurt. Occasionally, two men stay together because they love and need one another.*

The vast mass of men along Skid Row, U.S.A., however, are incapable of forming any love relationships with people. Still, there is a need for love in them, not so much to be loved, for they feel too unworthy, but to love somebody—or something. So they are notorious lonely-hearters who follow all the columns ranging from those appearing in their own Hobo News *to some in magazines like* Writer's Digest. *They write and receive letters and exchange pictures. They mull over the letters and dream over the pictures. Similarly, they vent their need for love on sexually significant objects. Flophouse keepers, who doubtless know more than anyone else about sex patterns here, say that there is no flop in this country which does not shelter its share of men whose most precious possessions are blouses or stockings or pieces of women's hair.*

A man named Robert Taylor, an old-time lodger at the

Red Star Hotel in Philadelphia, owns a vast number of down-at-the-heel women's shoes.

"See this guy Robert," a fellow lodger named Seymour Kraft said, while he, Robert, and I sat in the Red Star Saloon. "To look at him sitting here so dull, you wouldn't think he's got life in him. But if you saw him with a pair of white satin shoes he's got—oh boy!"

Robert took a sip of his wine and looked up at his friend.

"Can the kidding, pal," he said in a deliberately light and lilting voice. "You trying to make me out to be a shoe nut or something?"

Seymour said, "No."

Robert said, "What're you saying such a thing for then?"

"Because it's true," Seymour said.

Robert turned to me. He said he didn't know what shoes Seymour was talking about. Why, to listen to Seymour, one might think he hunted shoes in garbage cans from coast to coast.

Seymour said, "That's exactly what he does do."

Robert said, "I do not." He banged his hand on the table. "I don't do no such a thing." His face was flushed and still cadaverous-looking without the false teeth he usually wore, and his eyes shone black. "I do not. But suppose I did, would it be anybody's business?"

"No," Seymour said.

He turned to me. "Would it?"

I said, "No."

"O.K.," he said, "I got plenty of shoes then."

Pretty Pete was less defensive about his size 12 pink nylon slip. He pulled it out of his pocket while he and I sat in the Golden Bough Saloon in Chicago and showed it to me. It was very dirty.

"I wished I had a way to keep it clean," he said. "But I can't seem to find any. All the filthy flops I've got to go into."

Pretty Pete, who is in his middle thirties and who has lived along Skid Row since a few months before his eighteenth birthday, says he bought the slip for company. "It happens to remind me of the girl," he said.

I said, "Which girl, Pete?"

He smiled and opened his blue eyes wide. "Why, any girl."

I said, "Doesn't the slip remind you of some particular girl you once had?"

He said, "I never had a girl."

"Would you like to have a girl?" I asked.

He smiled. "Who wouldn't?" He folded his slip carefully and placed it back in his pocket.

"I always hated the stiffs," John Radclif, the manager of the Red Star told me. "Never felt sorry for them. I figured, listen, they made their own beds, nobody forces them to be alkies or rummies, if they don't like this life let them get the hell out of it. They can work like me, can't they?

"But when I saw them with the things lots of them keep around, why, then I started being sorry. It's sad seeing a guy treating a stinking old petticoat like it's a pretty girl with cologne on. The way some of these alkies treat their things, why, I guess a lot of women would be pretty happy if their husbands treated them that way.

"One time I saw an old fellow had a funny-looking black felt hat. I don't know where he got it, probably off some old fleabag who didn't want it any more. It was a terrible-looking hat. But he loved it like a mother. Some other bum stole it off of him. Or maybe he lost it. I don't think he could've lost it, though, not the kind of care he took of it. Well, he came crying to me, telling me about this black felt hat. I mean he was crying real tears.

"I said, 'Look, fellow, what do you want me to do? I didn't take your damn hat.' He says, 'I know. I know you're a good man wouldn't do such a thing. That's why I'm coming to you. Maybe you'll help me find it. I need your help so bad. You see,' he says, 'I can't live without my hat.' I'm no softie. But there was something about that bum. 'Please,' he says, 'I'll give you anything I got if you only help me find my hat.' I said, 'I'd like to help you, but I don't know how.' Well, he says I should search all the bums in the flop. I started laughing. The old man draws himself up and stops crying and says, 'If somebody just stole your life away, mister, I wouldn't be laughing at you.' He made me feel ashamed of myself because I laughed. That old man stayed in my flop a couple of months after he lost his hat. He was a different fellow, sad, like his life really was stole away. If that sounds crazy to you, go on and laugh."

I said, "It doesn't sound crazy."

He said, "No. No, it doesn't. Not when you get to know the fellows."

The object worship so prevalent along Skid Row, U.S.A., is only hard to understand before you come to know the peculiar make-up of these men. In a sense it is a compromise between their hopelessness and their awareness of reality, mixed with their need for love. The sickest among them fantasy while they caress the shoes and stockings and slips and hair and hide them under the itchy blankets on the cots and hold them next to their bare bodies. The fantasy represents reality to them.

Lonely-hearting is another type of fantasy that has come to represent reality along Skid Row, U.S.A. At one and the same time it makes allowance for Rowers' basic ineffectuality and still permits them to believe they are observing the norm of the strange and terrifying world outside. They can dream about possessing their lonely-hearts partners and still they need make no realistic advance toward them. Lonely-hearts communication is the fashion along Skid Row, U.S.A.

During the month of December 1954, nineteen men in Philadelphia's Red Star Hotel were engaged in avid lonely-hearts correspondence.

"That is, nineteen were known to me," the flop manager said. "They got so involved they'd keep pestering me about didn't I get a letter from their girls today. There's plenty more I don't know anything about. The men I get to know about are the ones who think they're in love with their letter-friends. Like this guy Martin Schatt's crazy about a girl called Roberta from some hick town in Michigan."

Martin Schatt is a man nearing sixty. He is tall and lanky, and he wears tight ballet dancer's pants that come down to a few inches above his ankles. He walks like a ballet dancer too, carefully, almost mincingly. He has a friend at a barber college in Philadelphia who keeps his black hair cut in a crew.

The first time Martin and I spoke about Roberta, his voice had a hushed quality. "Marilyn Monroe ain't got nothing this little girl don't have." He pulled a picture of her out of his pocket. "Look at them eyes. Them teeth. That hair."

The picture of Roberta showed a girl of eighteen or so with shoulder-length hair, a narrow forehead, and a pixie expression. Her figure was slender and, as Martin described it, "plenty stuffed in the right places."

Martin said, "My Roberta's smart, too. She's got the prettiest handwriting you ever saw. Don't you think I'm lucky to have found somebody like her?"

I said he was very lucky. "But," I added, "I don't understand why such a pretty girl would have to correspond with a man she doesn't know."

Martin said, "I think it's easy to understand. There's nobody but farmers out in Michigan. What would Roberta be wanting with a big galoot of a farmer? She needs a guy's been around big cities like New York, Chicago, Philadelphia, and Washington, D.C."

Roberta was pleased when Martin wrote and told her that he'd spent most of his life around big cities.

"It was the truth, too," he says. "I was glad to be able to tell her the truth about something. Most of the fellows sure lie when they write their girls."

"What do they lie about?" I asked.

"Oh, everything," he said. "The way they look. How old they are. They tell the girls they make good money on steady jobs. I done it myself. Roberta's sweet and I'm a rat. The lies I told that girl."

To begin with, he said, he had written Roberta that he had a steady job as a steel riveter—a steady job, mind you, he had said—he, who'd never worked a steady day in his life. And he hadn't had the moral scrupulousness to stop at that lie. Oh no, not Mrs. Schatt's little boy Martin. He had also written Roberta that he had graduated from four colleges. He, "an old dumb goat" who had never been past the fifth grade.

If I didn't think these two lies were glaring enough, what did I suppose he had done when Roberta had, naturally, requested a picture of him? Did I think he had been a decent fellow and had a picture made and just gone and sent it to her? Oh no. Just because he was a cheat and a liar at heart, he had felt forced to play around with her affections. He had solicited his tall, broad, good-looking Scotch friend, Angus, to pose for that picture.

I asked Martin whether he had thought what would happen if Roberta ever found out that he and Angus were different men.

"How the hell's she ever going to find out?" he asked. Martin Schatt, much as he adores his Roberta, never visualizes going beyond the exchange of letters he is engaging in presently. He dreams about her, of course, but he never confuses the dream with any possible reality. He knows when he comes down to facing facts that Michigan, U.S.A., and Skid Row, U.S.A., are two distinctly different worlds.

Only a very few Rowers manage to combine the two worlds. Loving women who never were of Skid Row serve as the bridges. For reasons of their own, they fall in love with these strange Rowers and try to deal with their perversities. But they do not have a chance. Their relationships are doomed. The men are bound to hurt them. The more the men hurt the women, the more they hate themselves. Since they need to hate themselves, they will go on hurting the women and hurting them until, finally, most of the women will feel forced to cry quits.

Samuel J. McKee is a Bowery habitué who has "shacked up" with a lady named Annie Clay. He is a "gandy-dancer" for the Pennsylvania Railroad during the spring and summer months. He divides his winter between the Bowery flops and the apartment of Annie Clay.

"I room and board with Annie," he says, "and I give her what she needs. She likes what I give her."

Annie Clay is a tall, angular woman. There is a scent of New England morality about her. Her skin is a dull beige color, and so is her thin hair. She just had her fortieth birthday.

Sammy McKee apologized for Annie Clay before he introduced me to her.

"She ain't no dreamboat for looks," he said.

I said, "There are plenty of things more important than looks."

Sammy nodded his bald head in agreement. "Yeah, like cooking." He placed his hand on his round, fat belly. "I could almost lose this when I'm on the road. But not when I'm back here with Annie. Can that bird cook. She's O.K. except one time she begun acting like we was married. She started making blah, blah, about me taking a bath. 'Please, Sammy,' she says, 'it'd be so nice if you was to smell nice in bed.' I told her no and she made me mad when she talked that way. So she said she was sorry and she wouldn't do it no more."

"Did she?" I asked.

"Hell, no," Sam said.

I first met Annie Clay at her apartment where Sammy brought me to dinner. She lived on East Ninth Street up five flights of very steep stairs.

I think Annie's apartment was the most spotless place I've ever seen. It was small, with an icebox placed in the bathroom and a combined living-bedroom perhaps ten by twelve feet. The wall was painted a bright salmon, and there were sheer white curtains on the one window.

I said, "Did you make these curtains, Annie? They're pretty."

Annie smiled thinly. Her hand, placed in mine when we were first introduced, felt cold.

"Not that they look homemade," I said.

Annie went on smiling. She did not look at me though.

I repeated, "Not that they look homemade. I should say they don't." I released her hand and picked up one of the curtains. "Isn't this hand stitching? It's lovely."

Annie stopped smiling. She looked straight at me. "Yeah," she said. "I made them. I worked two nights from nine o'clock till midnight."

I said, "I wish I could sew."

Annie smiled again. "I always sewed since I was a little girl."

"That's a talent," I said. "I'd be proud if I could sew like you."

"Proud? Well, I don't know about that," she said. "It's only sewing. Proud? Well, I don't know."

She was proud though. She went to one of the two cots that stood beside the window and removed a pink and blue hand-crocheted spread and brought it to me.

"This is something I did myself too, at nights, after work."

I said, "It's really lovely." I turned to Sammy. "Don't you think it's lovely?"

"Mmmm," Sammy said.

Annie looked down at it. "Pink and blue is nice together. I wasn't going to use this wool for a spread though. I had it a long time. I was going to use it for—if I ever had a little baby, you know, blue for a boy, pink for a girl."

Sammy grabbed hold of Annie's skinny arm. "You better can that. I don't want to hear no more talk about babies."

Annie said, "Don't get mad. I know I can't have babies, Sammy."

"All right," Sammy said. "All right. Just shut up then, that's all." I had never seen him so aroused.

Later, after he and I had left Annie's apartment, I told Sammy that I wondered why he didn't marry her and settle down and have a child.

"Me marry anybody?" he asked. "What the hell good would I be as a husband?"

I said, "Annie seems to think you're pretty good as a lover, Sammy."

"That's different," he said.

I said, "I don't think so. I think a man who's a good lover can be a good husband—if he wants to be."

"All right," he said, obviously eager to bring the conversation to a close, "so maybe I don't want to be."

I said, "Why not, Sammy? Annie's too good to let go. You'll never find another woman to love you the way she does."

"I don't care," he said. "Who wants to tie myself up to such a dumb ox?"

I said, "Sammy, why do you call Annie dumb?"

"Because she is," he said.

I persisted. "Why do you call her dumb?"

"Because."

"Because why?"

"Just because."

I said, "Sammy, I think you would call any woman who was in love with you dumb. Isn't that right?"

"It ain't wrong," he said.

I said, "Sammy, why?"

He said, "What does any woman want to love me for?"

I said, "Love doesn't come with reason, Sammy. Annie doesn't know why she loves you. She just loves you, that's all."

He smiled. "Sure. She's a dope, like I told you before."

I said, "Don't you love Annie at all, Sammy?"

He shook his head no. "I wouldn't've got messed up with her in the first place except she begged me to."

Annie Clay's relationship with Sammy McKee, the reason why a good, moral woman can live with a man like Sammy, cannot be understood without knowing about her life before Sammy came into it.

From the time she was a young child in Youngstown, Ohio, Annie Clay had considered herself the homeliest girl she knew. She'd had a stepmother who'd always told her that and a father who'd never contradicted it. Then, when she'd grown old enough to be interested in boys, circumstances had proved her stepmother right. No boy had ever paid any attention to her. Except one. His name was Meyer and he took her to the movies once. That was all the dates she'd ever had, one movie with a boy named Meyer.

When she was nineteen Annie Clay came to New York. She went to work in a dress factory and lived in a girls' club on Nineteenth Street. She didn't make many friends at the club, since most of the girls' lives centered around dating. There was one girl whom she did become friendly with, however. Her name was Molly Shay. She was a blowzy, overweight girl who never wore any make-up nor attempted to do anything about a badly pimpled skin, and Molly had no more dates than Annie did.

When Annie Clay was twenty-six, seven years after she had come to New York, she left the girls' club. She and Molly rented an apartment, the one on East Ninth Street. Molly was a very undomestic kind of girl who hated cooking and cleaning, and Annie was happy to assume all the domestic chores. She liked having someone to do for, and Molly was wonderful company. On Saturday nights they went to the movies together.

Annie says that maybe the best days of all with her friend were the times when Molly got sick and Annie had to take care of her. She felt so necessary to Molly's welfare then and therefore so warm and so good. She could have gone on forever, living with Molly in the happy companionship they had together.

Three years ago Molly had changed, though, not just toward her but in every way. First, she'd gotten some salve that had cleared all the sores off her face. Then she'd gone on a diet. And finally she had had her brown hair dyed blond.

On the day she became a blonde, Annie says, Molly became a different girl. She developed what she called a "new personality" to go with the blond hair and said that she just knew something important was going to happen to her.

After she became a blonde, Molly never felt like staying home. She was always dragging Annie out to bars.

One night, at a bar called "George's" in Greenwich Village, Molly flirted with a sailor. She told Annie she was not flirting either, cross her heart and hope to die, but Annie knew she was. The sailor knew too. He came over and asked Molly to dance. It upset Annie to see them dancing the way they were, too close together, and Molly's face so flushed.

Later, after Molly had danced a long time with her sailor, she told Annie not to wait for her, that she wasn't coming home that night, or maybe she wouldn't get back for a week or a month or a year, depending on her lovey-dovey sailor boy. She said that if Annie had the sense she was born with she wouldn't go home alone either.

After Molly and her sailor left, Annie stood looking around. She had no idea of taking Molly's advice—she'd been lonely before and she could envision being that way again. It was just something about Sammy, when she saw him standing at the far end of the bar.

She approached him. "I ain't a bad woman," she said. "I never did anything like this before. I know it's very late, and you must've had supper. But it's so late, maybe you're ready for some more."

"Huh?" Sammy asked.

Annie said, "I can cook real good."

Sammy McKee describes his first meeting with Annie pretty much the way she does. He says he had just hit town that night after a "gandy-dancing" season and he had a bulging roll in his pocket.

"I wanted somebody," he says, "and I felt kind of sorry for Annie being such a funny-looking fool. Besides, I was hungry. I figured I'd eat with her and then go on home."

Annie cooked a wonderful dinner.

"Well, s'long," Sammy told her after he'd finished eating. "I got to be going, I guess."

"Yes," she answered, "sure."

But there had been that expression in Annie Clay's eyes. Sammy felt that he owed her something for her hospitality. So he kissed her.

"I didn't feel like it," he says, "but what was I going to do after eating up all that hamburger she gave me?"

The kiss that had begun as casually as that for Sammy McKee didn't end that way. Annie Clay responded so passionately that he could not remain casual. He kissed her again. And he stayed with her that night.

In the morning, Sammy woke up first. He looked at Annie sleeping, her thin hair sloppy on the pillow, her mouth half open.

"She's a ugly thing," he says he told himself. He jumped out of bed and hurried to put on his clothes so that he wouldn't have to talk to her again.

But Annie woke before he could leave. She smiled at him and pulled the covers tight around her long, skinny body.

"Please," she said, "turn your head the other way." Then she added tentatively, "Sweetheart."

Sammy McKee is a little ashamed of what happened next. Telling about it now, he says, "That word, sweetheart, the way she was saying it. I figured what the hell was the skinny hank of hair and dried-up bones trying to do anyways—tie me down? The word sweetheart didn't hurt my feelings. Nothing wrong with sweetheart. It's a good word, but when Annie said it I got mad as a peed-off pile driver. I told her, 'Don't call me no names!' She started in crying. Boy, is she nutty-looking when she cries. So I told her I was sorry for hurting her feelings."

Annie begged Sammy to stay for breakfast, and he figured he might as well. After breakfast she went down and brought up a *Daily News* for him. She suggested that he return to bed for a while. Surely he must be tired after—last night. She herself had to go to work. She was late already. There was one thing she had to tell Sammy McKee before she went. She had never felt so alive before. She was grateful for what he had done for her. She would never forget him.

Sammy McKee does not admit it, but as he tells his story today you know that he was moved by Annie in spite of himself. This was the first time in *his* life in a sense, as well as in Annie's. For when had any woman before implied that his love-making meant something to her? He said that he might possibly be around when she came back from work.

That would be wonderful, Annie assured him. If she could expect him, she would shop on her way home from work and cook him the best dinner he'd ever eaten.

Annie and Sammy had steak for their dinner. They washed it down with red wine an Italian girl who worked in Annie's shop had given her once.

"That night we went back to bed together," Sammy says.

And so Annie Clay and Sammy McKee have been lovers for three years, off and on. But both of them know the relationship cannot last.

"Sometimes I hate her guts because she takes so much off me," he says. "I knock her down on the floor and slap her around with my fists. After she gets up she says she loves me."

Someday Annie Clay will get up off the floor and neglect to tell Sammy she loves him. He'll walk out of her life that day, convinced she kicked him out because he wasn't good enough. And when he gets back on to the Row, he'll join his cohorts in fantasy living, and Annie Clay, when he describes her to them, will be a brilliant beauty with a strong mind of her own, alas.

I know a few men along Skid Row, U.S.A., who started out with transient love relationships with good women and ended up husbands, because the women were masochistic enough to go on tolerating all the evil treatment the men gave them. But the majority of women who become involved with Rowers are like Annie Clay, desperately lonely, inferior-feeling themselves, but not masochistic. So they have to give up after a while. And the men return to their unattached lives and try to persuade themselves that they are hunting for new attachments.

But they know inside of them that they will do their best to avoid new attachments and not seek them out. They know that the fact that they prefer "burleycue gals" and prostitutes to good women is a form of avoidance. They wouldn't have known it before they experienced the love of the good women in their lives, but they do know it now. The good women were ready to give to them, and the "burleycue gals" and prostitutes make no pretense of wanting to do anything but take from them. The "burleycue gals" tell them straight out that all they want are a few weeks or months of luxury living and whatever presents they can promote for themselves. The live ones among the prostitutes cannot afford to be quite so blatantly demanding, but they make strong demands, too.

Miss Pansy Lee Carter is a sort of lady idol along Skid Row, U.S.A. She is a study in female contradictoriness, for, although she bumps for a living, she is happiest when with a colorful apron tied around her ample middle she is cooking up a new dish. Bumping may be her profession, but creative cooking is her mode of self-expression.

I was aware of Pansy Lee's proclivity for cooking before I met her for the first time in Longchamps's Restaurant on Fifth Avenue in New York. She told me about it on the telephone when I called her to arrange an appointment. She also described herself to me.

"A few people call me—well—sexy," she said.

Her description was an understatement. She oozed sex as she sat at a Longchamps's table for two. Emily Post would not have approved the way she held her legs, slim at the ankles, almost too fat at the calves, but the three men within gaping distance of her could not manage to keep their eyes on their respective women.

Looking at those legs myself, I approached her table and said, "You must be Pansy Lee Carter."

"Yes, why, yes, yes, yes, I am." She stuck a soft white hand into mine. "I'm Pansy Lee. And you recognized me right off the bat. You're a dream to do that. How did you manage anyhow?"

"One of your admirers described you to me," I said.

"How nice of him," she said. "Or maybe it wasn't a him at all. It could have been a woman for all I know."

"It was not a woman," I said.

"Yes, well, sure, I guess not. I don't know too many of them." The way she said "them" made women sound like a species from some other planet who swooped down her way once in a while.

After three daiquiris, a steak sandwich, and two helpings of French pastry, I felt unloosed to the point where I could approach Pansy Lee about her relationship with Skid Row men.

"You know," I said tentatively, "you're sort of a dreamboat on the Bowery."

She smiled. "Yes. The men throng where I happen to be playing in whichever theater. I feel very sorry for them. When they get rolls they always want to spend them up on little old me. I can't think why. One time there was a fellow named Pete Miloo who brought back five hundred dollars after working for eight months out in Casper,

Wyoming. He started waiting outside of my theater for me three days in a row. I walked right past, because I didn't like the way he looked. Once he caught up with me, held my arm so I got so frightened I couldn't scream out for anybody to help me, and then just forced his old money on me."

"What did you do then?" I asked.

Pansy Lee smiled. "What *could* I do?"

Pansy Lee Carter was not shy about admitting that she often "took on" generous Rowers like Pete Miloo—"only those who got the biggest rolls, of course." She said it was not just Rowers' money that attracted her, either.

"I don't have to have men like Miloo," she said. "I could get men with real fortunes. But they don't behave very well. They want to keep me someplace and come to see me when they take time off from their wives, and most of the time they're with me they're wondering how they can be such a heel to their wives and supposing somebody was to find out. They're just scaredy-cats. Pete Miloo and these other guys are different. They pay a girl good. Still and all, they respect me. Whatever I do is O.K., and they think I'm doing them a big favor."

I said, "Maybe they respect you, but they don't respect themselves."

"I know that," she said. In her own way she is aware of the Skid Row man's egolessness, and she uses it for her purposes. But she doesn't feel she is misusing it. She is happy, and the Skid Row men she knows are happy when they are with her.

"You just don't know how many men come around offering me presents when they have rolls in their pockets," she said. "Sometimes they'll give me two hundred dollars without even expecting me to kiss and squeeze and get in bed with them. They're so good to me I sometimes think I'd like to make them happy for free."

Skid Row men who have experienced the favors of burlesque girls live for the times when they can afford them again. Not that I ever spoke to a single one of them who even dreamed of taking a full-time job so that he might win a permanent mistress from among the ranks of the "burleycue gals." He wouldn't want one. The "burleycue gals" attract him because they are unattainable for permanent living.

Skid Rowers prefer to be part of a woman's menage, not her one and only. That is one reason why those who cannot aspire to "burleycue gals" can sometimes become sentimental over prostitutes.

Edgar, a skinny, white-haired Bowery old-timer, considers himself madly in love with a thirty-year-old, flabby, dark-haired live one named Marva Stringer.

"She makes me crazy," he says. "I had three nice women once upon a time. They'd go to work for me and do anything I wanted. They never worried me. I don't know why I carry a torch for Marva. The things she makes me do. Oh, you'd be surprised. She makes me go out and find her men. Be a pimp for her. She says, 'You can smell a guy with a roll a mile away. All you have to do is bring him to me.' Don't you think it's terrible for a man's own girl to make him pimp for her?"

I said, "Yes, Edgar."

"Well," he said, "a lot of live ones makes their boy friends pimp around for them."

"What do the boy friends get out of it?" I asked.

Edgar smiled. "A heartache, ma'am."

"Why do you stay with Marva?" I asked.

Edgar didn't answer my question for a long time. Then, when I thought he wasn't going to answer it at all, he said, "If it wasn't Marva or somebody like her, who *could* it be? A filthy fleabag? I'd know I was really finished then. I get goose flesh when I look in their faces."

Fleabags, even along tolerant Skid Row, U.S.A., are condemned as the lowest women who walk the streets. They have lost all semblance of femininity, and yet they consciously strive to be female. They primp and preen and admire themselves in cracked saloon mirrors, and they constantly try to persuade themselves that the truth is a lie and that they are desirable women. They use the men who are forced to "go with them" as props to bolster their egos. Skid Rowers who are adept at offering rosy compliments can secure fleabags' favors for less money than they would have had to pay without the compliments.

Take the case of Stinky McGee who solicited a fleabag named Baldy Mary outside the Red Star in Philadelphia. Stinky is a smallish old-timer, and Mary is a hefty woman in her sixties with a bald head.

"Well," Stinky asked, "how much?"

"A dollar seventy-five," Mary said.

"You're loony," Stinky said.

Mary grew thoughtful. "How's $1.50?"

"Never."

"How come?"

"For $1.50 I could get a movie star."

"Like hell you could."

"I could too."

"So if you can get a movie star," Mary asked, "what are you barking at me for?"

"I like you."

"Yeah?"

"Sure."

"How much?"

"Plenty."

Mary looked triumphant. "Do you like me $1.50's worth?" she asked craftily.

"Sure I like you $1.50's worth. Only I ain't got $1.50."

"How much you got?"

"Fifteen cents."

Mary said, "Drop dead."

Stinky said, "I like you better than a movie star."

Baldy Mary looked into his eyes. "You're kidding."

Stinky said, "No. No, Mary. Honest."

Baldy Mary went with Stinky McGee for fifteen cents.

"I really can't stomach the way fleabags makes you say they're wonderful," Stinky told me later. "But you got to do what they want. You look in a pair of red eyes and you got to say they're gorgeous. You feel like a dope, but what

can you do when you ain't got enough money to pay for a
live one? Live ones get anyplace between $1.75 and $5.
Where can I get that kind of money? I'd have to be without a woman six months. Some fellows can do it. I can't.
I ain't built right to. I got to have a woman, so I go ahead
and get the best I can afford. Sometimes I don't look at
fleabags I go with. I feel sick to think I am forced to lead
this kind of life like men in prisons. If I ever get on my
feet again, I will get married and go on relief. I thought
I was doing right staying single. I see now that that's
crazy. I should have got some girl before I got to look this
way and married her. Then I wouldn't be forced to look
fleabags up. I wish I could wait for a woman longer than
I can. Then I could save up my money and go to a live
one."

Stinky McGee generally pays twenty to fifty cents to
fleabags whom he can't flatter into taking less.

"I guess I'll get sick off fleabags and die someday," he
says. "As it is one of them stole my false teeth. I got all
my teeth knocked out in a accident thirteen years ago, and
the money I got out of it paid for this set of false ones.
They were beautiful. I'd still have them if it wasn't for
this fleabag named Lila. She got me down a dark cellar
she lived in. She had some kind of drapery stuff hung all
over the place. I asked how she come to have it hung all
over. She said, 'Don't worry. I only hung them because
my astrologer told me to!' I believed her and we arranged
on the price, thirty-nine cents, and then she said I should

163

make myself comfortable, take out my teeth, and put them in a glass of water she would get for me."

Stinky McGee followed Lila's suggestion about his false teeth. He did feel more comfortable without them.

"I could've relaxed," he said, "if it hadn't been so dark in that cellar, so I asked her why she didn't turn a light on."

Lila replied that love was better in the dark. Remembering how she had looked to him in daylight, he was inclined to agree with her.

"After we finished our business, I started looking for my teeth," he says. "First, I felt around for the glass I put them in. That was there all right, but when I felt around for the teeth in the glass, why, then there weren't any."

Stinky did not accuse Lila outright. He only suggested that he would appreciate her assistance in locating the lost teeth.

"Teeth?" Lila asked. "What teeth?"

Stinky began to plead with her. "Give me back my teeth, Lila."

She said, "You never owned teeth."

There was nothing for Stinky McGee to do then, except to return to the saloon his friends always hung out in.

"Look at me," he said to one of the friends.

The friend said, "What's the matter?"

"My teeth," Stinky said. "They're gone."

"Teeth?" the friend asked, as Lila, the fleabag, had asked before him. "What teeth?"

He was only joking, but Stinky had no way of knowing

it, so he broke down and cried. A policeman came around and saw him crying and pulled him into court for disturbing the peace.

Stinky tried to enlist the judge's interest in the matter of the false teeth. But the judge only laughed at him and said he should have known better than to go to a fleabag.

"I have to admit the judge was right in a way," Stinky said. "Fleabags smells on ice, and if I had any sense I'd never have a thing to do with them. I'd get a nice little boy friend instead."

Many Skid Rowers have taken "little boy friends," primarily because they could not tolerate fleabags.

"Why not?" asked an intelligent Chicago Rower called Crippy, because he has a clubfoot. "Even outcasts have to have some kind of life, don't they? Some of us find fleabags repulsive. But we've got to get love some way. This is the only way open to us."

Many Rowers who engage in homosexual activity do not fool themselves into regarding it as anything but a love substitute. They get together for mutual relief, and they don't mind letting each other know it. Some of them go in for "one-night stands" and some for combinations that last as long as they are convenient for both parties. Jockers and punks feel a certain loyalty to one another as long as they stay together. But they are distinctly casual on the whole.

"I used to have a boy friend named Mike," a forty-one-year-old Philadelphian told me, "till yesterday when he went and left me."

I said, "Do you miss him?"

He said, "I guess."

I said, "Where did he go?"

He said, "How'd I know?"

I said, "Didn't he tell you?"

"Why should he tell me where he goes?" he asked.

I met many Skid Rowers who were practicing homo-sexuals, and only one of them, a forty-seven-year-old New-arker named Mike Anderson, ever seemed to care very much about his paramour.

I first saw Mike Anderson in a Newark courtroom. He was a small, slight, bald man with a bloodied-up nose and a black eye.

"You were fighting?" the judge asked him.

"Yes, your honor."

"Why?"

"I couldn't tell in court, sir. Somebody else'd be hurt if I did."

I bought him coffee after the judge released him. I sug-gested he go to the men's room and wash the blood off his nose and that we go to a drug store and try to get something for the black eye.

"I don't want to wash the blood or treat the eye," he said. "Thanking you for your kindness all the same."

I said, "You'll look better when you're washed and treated."

He smiled. "Not to my little punk I won't. I want him to see me looking this way. Maybe he'll feel sorry and come back to me."

I said, "Your punk?"

His voice softened. "Yeah, my punk. He's the sweetest little fellow."

I said, "How old is he?"

"Thirty-one," he said. "We were together sixteen years. I picked him up in a little hick town, and he's been mine ever since. I never looked at anybody else. Neither did he —before this."

"What's your punk's name?" I asked.

He said, "I always called him 'Honey Boy.' We used to spend a lot of time on the road when we first met. We didn't like city flops, because we couldn't be together the way we wanted." His voice broke. "I wish we'd stayed in the country all the time. I wish we never had come to those rotten city flops. Then there wouldn't have been all those wolves who were just waiting to get their paws on my Honey Boy."

"A city wolf took Honey Boy from you?" I asked.

He began to cry. "That's right. Tempted him away from me. He had more money, and he offered him a real room to sleep in. Honey Boy never had a real room. So he went with him. But I keep hanging around outside their flop. I want to be around if anything happens."

Mike Anderson has become a laugh along Skid Row, Newark. His cohorts cannot understand why he should feel the way he does about one little punk. They often ridicule his maudlin devotion.

"Mike was a real nut to keep a punk for fifteen years," Dickie Crystal told me.

Dickie Crystal, forty-three years old, owner of a highly pawnable silver watch and chain, always compares Mike's relationship with Honey Boy to his own relationship with other punks.

"Believe me, I had plenty of kids myself," he says. "I still do. All my punks were cuter'n that moron kid of Mike's. But I never got so crazy about any of them. What for? A kid says he's leaving me, I tell him O.K., good luck."

Dickie says he never had an affair that lasted more than a few months. Some of them were over in a few days.

"My long affairs only happened while I was on the road. A punk's nice when you're traveling. He's company. It's different in cities. There, somebody dragging on your tail is not so good. So what I do in cities is come up to a cute fellow plain and open and tell him what I want. If he wants the same thing, good. If not——" He shrugged. "My feelings don't get hurt if a fellow tells me no. Way I figure, there'll always be another fellow to tell me yes."

There usually is. For the kind of an affair Dickie suggests can eliminate loneliness temporarily. In a sense it is the most satisfying sex pattern open to these men, not inanimate as a woman's petticoat, nor far away as a lonely-heart correspondent, not disgusting as a fleabag when the men have to see her straight, or cruel as a live one often is, not expensive as a "burleycue gal," or demanding as a good woman might be.

7. Hobohemia, U.S.A.

Genuine hobos are among the fringe people of Skid Row, U.S.A. They are all old men in their seventies and eighties and nineties, remainders out of another era. They were wandering workers from about 1870 to about 1922 and were necessary adjuncts to the development of this country. In their day, they cut down trees in the great north forests, built roads and railroads, worked as cutters in the ice harvests and as mule and horse drivers during the days of horsepower construction.

There are very few genuine hobos still alive, and those who are are remnants of what they once used to be. No jobs any more, even for the young, healthy men of their type, and certainly none for the sick old men they are today.

"Mine whole heart cries for the men used to be hobos," Schloime the Troime told me over lunch at the Bluebird Cafeteria on Delancey Street. "What fine fellows they was. Not bums and that's the honest and true. They was brave, good men when they was young. You see them today, maybe you can't know they was good. You got to talk to them to find out. Maybe it'll take a long time before they should let you know they're fine fellows. Nu, so, let it take. It'll be worth it by you. I wish I could give you the pleasure you should meet a couple hobos by name 'Hoime the Horse' and also 'Pick Shovel Kid.' I'm very sorry I should have to tell you they dropped down dead and can't meet nobody no more. Still and all I'm very glad I can give you the big pleasure you should have a meeting with Rickety Stan and Cussin' Cassidy and a very nice boy his name is Big Belly Bob."

Schloime introduced Cussin' Cassidy and me in the Bluebird Cafeteria. Cussin' grinned toothlessly when I asked him how he came to hit the road. He said, "I was born on a farm. I got too much guts to stay on it and be a 'scissor-bill.' In case you don't know it, a 'scissor-bill' is a dumb, stay-to-home farmer. Not for me. Aw no. Well, see, I was a son with itching feet. I didn't want to be a city homeguard neither. A homeguard is a guy hangs around one city and don't give a hoot in hell if he ever makes it out or not. That wasn't no life for old Cussin' Cassidy. Look me over. Do I look like a homeguard to you?"

I looked him over. He was a small man with a bald head that was too big for his body. He looked older than the sixty-one years he admitted to. He had weak eyes, and he kept shutting them to keep the light out of them.

"No," I said, "you don't look like a homeguard to me, Cussin'."

He grinned again. "Well, goddamn," he said, "what do you know about that? Sixty-one years and I still don't look like no homeguard." Then he regarded me consideringly. "I guess I could've been one. If things was different. See, I came off the farm I was born on and I went to Chicago to work. It's a funny thing about me and work. The work I wanted never wanted me. I wasn't good enough for a good, clean job. I would've took any nice, clean job in those days. There weren't nice, clean jobs for nobody like me. Aw no. Cussin' Cassidy wants to work, you know what he got to do, work twelve, fourteen hours a day for nothing. What kind of life's that?"

Cussin' was sixteen years old when he left the farm and came to Chicago and got a job in the slaughter industry there.

"You know what," he says, "my whole family came. Me, my two brothers, and my little sister went right to work. The bastard stockyards! What a stink. I used to vomit up my guts trying to get rid of it. Me and my family worked all week, Sundays too. We was religious when we first came off the farm." He smiled to himself. "Yeah, no kidding, I used to go for all that God mess. I'm telling you I was a kind of a dumb kid. Whatever the preachers said was O.K. with me. Well, anyways, what I started to tell you, poor son of a bitch works on Sundays he can't go to church. So one time I went up to one of the baby bosses, see? He wasn't no big shot. There was plenty of bigger bosses over him. I told him how I wanted to go to church. He punched me in the nose. I said, 'Look, what the hell

171

did you do that for?' He said, 'Just to show you who's boss!' Well, how you think that made me feel?" He looked at me. "How you think, huh? You think it made me feel good or lousy?"

I said, "Lousy, Cussin'."

"If something like that happened to you," he asked, "what would you do? Punch him back, maybe?"

I said, "Well, Cussin'——"

He said, "Punch him back, yeah, yeah. When you're a worker, you can't punch the boss back. He'd kill you and the police would back him up. Workers are animals in this world." He hesitated a moment. Then he smiled. "You know what workers got heads for? Do you?"

"What for, Cussin'?" I asked.

"For the bastard bosses to crap on," he answered.

That statement was echoed one way or another by almost every former hobo in Cussin's age group. Everyone I spoke to talked the same way.

"This is a stinking country for workingmen."

"I hate this lousy America. Mr. Rockefeller and them other bosses care more about their ratty hounds 'n they do about workers."

"What do they care if you drop dead in their shops? Workers are cheap in this country. Somebody else is always around to take your place."

"Before I started beating my way on the road I was a good worker just like anybody. I used to work my head off. Well, you know how much money I made. Sixteen cents an hour."

Cussin' Cassidy and his generation worked in American industry during the early 1900's when government reporters stated that the average income in Chicago slaughter was $6.37 a week and that employees in coal mining had to expect to be unemployed for one third to one half of the year and that one out of every ten working-class families had an annual income of less than $300 a year.

"From the day me and my folks first came to Chicago," Cussin' Cassidy tells, "we didn't know anybody wasn't beat and hungry all of the time. I ain't kidding. I bet you think I am, don't you?"

I said, "No, Cussin'."

He said, "You do bad things when you're beat and hungry." He turned away from me and looked down at his hands. He asked, "Do you believe that or do you think I'm full of crap?"

I said, "Sure, I believe it."

"Well, then," he seemed to be studying his words carefully, "I want to tell you something if you want to hear it."

I said, "I want to hear it very much."

He said, "It's about my sister. That O.K. with you?"

I nodded.

"She was a good girl," he said.

I said, "Yes."

Cussin' looked up from his hands. "Look, I want you to understand one thing before I tell you anything. She was a good girl. It don't matter what she done on the

173

outside. Inside she was good. A girl can be bad outside and good in her. You get it?"

I said, "Yes, Cussin'."

He said, "The bastard bosses were more to blame than her. Now you think I'm full of crap?"

I said, "No, Cussin'."

"Well, she started sleeping around when she was fifteen," he said. "Was she a pretty kid! A guy'd look at her. He'd want to get her. She was just off the farm and didn't know much. All she knew, she hated the stockyard stink. She had a cute little nose, my old man used to say it was kind of like a button, see, and I remember how cute she used to wrinkle it up soon's we got to the yards in the morning. One morning we all got there, she says, 'Pa, I ain't going to work this morning.' My old man says, 'Yeah, you're going all right. What's the matter with you anyways? You going crazy or something? We all got to work if we want to eat.' Poor Pa. I seen his face when he talked to my sister. I never saw anything like the way he looked. I don't know. You ever seen a dog after some son of a bitch kicked him in the face? That was my pa. It made me want to die to look at him. You understand what I mean?"

I said, "I think I do, Cussin'."

He tried to smile. "My pa loved all his kids, but he loved my little sister more'n the rest. So it made him feel lousy to tell her she got to go to work. She got mad. She said, 'Listen, Pa, I don't have to do nothing I don't want no more.' My pa got mad too and socked her one. Well, she looked at him like he was nothing and walked away.

My ma got hysterical. She said, 'What if we don't see her no more? It'll be your fault,' she said to my pa. He tried to get her to stop bawling, but she wouldn't do it so he said, 'I don't mind telling you I'll sock you too. Stop crying!' My ma said, 'I'll stop. I'll stop when my little baby comes home!'"

Cussin's sister never did come home. She went to live with a man she'd met at the yards.

"Goddamn son of a bitch," Cussin' tells. "First when I found out what my sister was doing I wanted to beat her brains out. But after a while, when I started thinking everything over why she had to do what she done and I thought to myself, 'She got guts. Yes, sir, that kid got more guts than me. You work in stink twelve hours every day, after a while you begin to think you're part of the stink yourself. Only one time in every worker's life maybe he'll get a idea the way my little sister done. I got to get out of this stink. It don't matter what else I do, go lay somebody, go out on the road, anything. You understand what I mean? Do you?"

I said, "I think so, Cussin'."

He put his hands over his eyes. "If you understand why my little sister went rotten, then you'll know what made me run. I started out on the road a few months after my sister left home. I was seventeen years old."

I said, "Where'd you go?"

Cussin' laughed. "I beat my way all over the country. I bet you I been to any town you can mention. I used to ride the rails. You think it was a easy life?"

175

I said, "I'm sure it wasn't."

He said, "I hated the life from the day I started it. Not the life exactly but the work and the way them bosses always took advantage of us guys because we didn't have no way to help ourselves. I got to California after beating the rails a year. All the other 'bos told me, 'California, boy, that's the place, sunshine and honey, maybe things is tough here but wait'll you hit California, you'll be glad you come out on the road.' Glad? Hoo! You want to know what happened once I hit California?"

I said, "Oh yes, Cussin'."

He said, "Well, the first year I was there, I got there in the summer, see, around July. I went right out to where them fish canneries were. A man took me in. He said, 'O.K., 'bo, you look plenty strong, good muscles, you got yourself a job.' Every day I went to work, see! You think I should've been eating good, ain't it?"

I said, "Yes, Cussin'."

"Well, I didn't," he said, "I never made enough of the old green stuff. I got me a lousy room reminded me of where I used to live in Chicago with my family and I ate good on payday, one day a week. After the summer was finished, I didn't do that no more neither. I got canned from the cannery." He laughed at his joke. "Hey, that's a good one, ain't it? 'Canned from the cannery.' So after I got canned from the cannery I went looking up another job. I couldn't find none. Everybody told me, 'Come back next summer, 'bo. Don't forget to come on back next summer. We can sure use you then.' I said, 'Yeah, that's great asking me to come back next summer. What about if I drop dead before I can get back?' What did they think I was going to do all winter? How'd they expect me to get along anyways?"

He got along during his first winter in California by doing odd jobs and alternating between ten- and fifteen-cent flops in Los Angeles and San Francisco.

"Today's flops ain't nothing to rave about," he says. "But in them days they was worse. Take this one house I still remember. They used to let you sleep on shelfs that were built all around the room for a nickel. Also, you could sleep on a bench or else on the floor. Sometimes my body got so sore, I used to spend a extra two cents. They used to charge seven cents for a hammock. Well, believe it or not except for the hammock, things was as crummy on the seven-cent floor as they was on the nickel one. There wasn't no towels on the seven-cent floor. Ain't that something? There was only one sink there too. It was sure filthy. Fifty, sixty, seventy guys used it all the time. They got no soap. Everybody stunk." He stopped. "I want to tell you something," he said, "I hope you won't be like them other writers say hobos is dirty. I wonder how clean they'd be theirselves if they lived in a dive like I done. Not just me. Millions of fellows. I tell you there was millions of men in them flophouses."

There *were* many thousands. During the winters of the early 1900's, according to a government report issued in 1913, more than forty thousand unemployed migratory workers lived in the San Francisco flops, while at least twenty-five thousand lived in the Los Angeles ones on a "winter's stake" estimated to be thirty dollars or thereabouts.

"You can't imagine how glad I was when summer come along and I could get out and get me some work," Cussin' said. "Well, I got work O.K. I picked out some jobs to take. What holes. Most places I slept out in the fields on piles of hay. There wasn't no toilets for us workers. Compared to the smell of them California farms, them Chicago slaughterhouses was real cologne factories. Sometimes it'd get hot in the fields and the bosses never sent us water to drink. Some men was married and had their little kids out there used to beg for water for the babies. What was they asking for anyways? A million bucks? All they begged for was water for the kids. But the bosses wouldn't send it. They rather *sell* us lemonade. You know another stinking thing they used to do. They used to switch pay signs on you. Say a sign goes up saying they was paying ninety cents for picking a hundred pounds of hop. O.K. The workers get in line waiting for jobs and let's say there's a lot of them that day. That's all the bosses got to see. Next thing you know the ninety cent sign's down and a new sign's up, saying they're paying eighty-five cents now. You never knew what they was going to be paying you from one day to the next one. So I decided to get the hell out of California. I might as well have stayed there for all the good I done myself. Everyplace else was just as lousy."

"Where else did you go?" I asked.

"All over the goddamn country," Cussin' said, "like I told you before. I worked in the lumber camps. Boy, the same kind of crap went on there. We never had enough blankets to cover with. Sometimes a couple of guys used to start sleeping together just to keep warm and then, since they had to lay close, they started in doing things. Them bosses made fairies out of nice boys. You think I'm crazy when I say that?"

I said, "No, Cussin'."

He said, "And they made bums out of smart fellows like me. I was born smart. Ma used to say I was the smartest one in my family. Why'd I have to go and become a bum then? Only because I couldn't stand that stockyard stink and had to run away from it. Then I had to keep on running because I couldn't find a decent job no place. I didn't ask for much out of a job. All I wanted was a chance to make enough so's I could eat and sleep good and maybe get married or send a few cents to my family. Then again I wanted to work in a place where the boss wouldn't treat me like dirt. There was no jobs like that. Them bosses is responsible for me being a bum."

Almost all the old-time hobos I met talked the way Cussin' Cassidy did. They held the "bastard bosses" to blame for all their misfortunes. They are different from the majority of Rowers in that they are neither egoless nor emotionless. On the contrary. Most of them feel that they have been deprived of their birthrights and so they are robustly class-conscious. And they have an amazing knowledge of the economics of the period that produced

179

them. Schloime the Troime, for example, has memorized most of the government reports relating to the economics of the early 1900's. He talks knowingly about widespread unemployment and the difficulties of working seasonal jobs. And he discusses conditions that were prevalent in the migrant labor camps all over the country.

"Things was terrible," he says. "Them bosses' hearts was made up from rusty iron. Say some workingmen had a argument with the bosses, the bosses was not worrying. By them in the head they had it figured out was always plenty men would work for nothing and never give the boss no arguments neither. They thought dumb workers was the cheapest things in the world. Till one time the dumb workers begun to get smart and says to each other, 'Alone we ain't nothing but weakers.' So what's to do, ha? Nothing? Nothing like hell! Is plenty to do. Is get together and organize a union. We won't be weakers no more if we got our own union. So the hobo workers organized and we got us the one big union."

"The one big union" was the IWW, the Industrial Workers of the World. It was born in the winter of 1905 along the main stem of Chicago and nurtured there in the flops and greasies and low-down saloons by itinerant workers who had come to "hole up" after working all summer and fall. Originally conceived to substitute industrial unions of unskilled workers for the trade unions of the American Federation of Labor, which had largely limited its membership to skilled people, it sought to combine all workers, agricultural and industrial, metalmen, lumbermen, railroaders and construction men into "one big union." Theoretically, it did not differentiate between migratories and stay-at-homers, but in actuality it began, almost from the day of its inception, to service the migratories primarily. Its membership was fluctuating, rising in the summer and falling in the winter, and there were as many as one hundred thousand members during the peak periods of the early 1900's.

Schloime the Troime says that the IWW had more than one hundred thousand members.

"By the capitalists, theirselves, they say one hundred thousand. Oy, what liars."

I said, "Schloime, how many members would you say there were?"

He narrowed his eyes and tapped his hand against his forehead. "Let me give it a little think," he said. "By me, I want to be sure I ain't getting you off wrong. The way I remember today, we used to have three, four million members." He smiled. "I ask you who's telling lies now? Who? Me, that's who. You should excuse it, please. The three, four million members was by me in the dream. Because I used to love that organization. Tell me, did you ever love a organization yourself?"

I said, "No, Schloime, I don't think I ever did. Not in the way you seem to have loved the IWW."

He smiled. "Is all right. Don't apologize. By you was never necessary you should love organizations. All the time you had plenty people in your life you should give your love to them. By me and the other hobos, we was not so lucky we should have people to love so that was why we *had* to love our organization. What I mean, by us was the one big union the only family we had. I want you should meet a fine fellow by the name Rickety Stan. He was also a lover from the one big union because was no people around in his life that he should give his love to them."

When I met Rickety Stan at the Sunshine Bar on the Bowery, I discovered that he had indeed been a passionate lover of his organization and that his love had lasted through the years. He was eighty years old, a toothpick of a man in a Salvation Army suit that swam on him, and he banged his small, wizened fist on the table in happy emphasis of everything he told me.

"Yeah, sure Schloime's right when he tells you I loved my union better'n anything in the world. Why wouldn't I anyways? Before it came, I never even knew I was a man. All the things I had to take off the bosses! 'Yes, sir. No, sir. Anything you say, sir.' My organization sure changed things. After it got organized, I could tell my bosses to go to hell."

When the IWW was organized in 1905 Rickety Stan was twenty years old and he had been all over this country several times. He'd picked fruit, harvested wheat, worked on railroads, and done lumbering.

"Never did find a place to lay my head steady before my union came," he said. "No matter where I was working, things'd always get so bad I'd have to move on. After my union, I didn't have to move no more unless I wanted to. If things got bad, I could stay right where I was and fight the bosses was making them bad. My union brothers would help me. I never felt like a brother to no man or woman till after I joined the one big union. Before I'd thought I was nothing but a bum. After I got in our union, I found out who the real bums was. Not me and my brothers but the bosses we was working for. We used to have a poem about that. You want to hear it?"

I said, "Oh yes."

He said, "I got to stand up on a chair in order to recite it right."

He stood up and I helped him get on to a chair. He stood up straight and placed his right hand on his heart.

"The name of this poem is, 'The Bum on the Plush and the Bum on the Rods.'

    "The bum on the rods is hunted down
      As the enemy of mankind
      The other is driven around to his club,
      Is feted and wined and dined,
      And they who curse the bum on the rods,
      As the essence of all that is bad
      Will greet the other with a winning smile,
      And extend the hand so glad."

He stopped reciting. He looked at me with his red-rimmed eyes. "Get it?" he asked.

I said, "Yes, I do."

"Well, what does it mean to you anyways?"

I said, "It means that while the poor man who has to hobo his way from job to job is disapproved of, the rich

183

man, regardless of what methods he has used to make money, is catered to."

He regarded me with real approval. "You get it," he said. "Here's the second part."

"The bum on the rods is a social flea,
Who gets an occasional bite,
The bum on the plush is a social leech,
Bloodsucking day and night.
The bum on the rod is a load so light
That his weight we scarcely feel,
But it takes the labor of dozens of men,
To furnish the other a meal.
As long as you sanction the bum on the plush
The other will always be there
But rid yourself of the bum on the plush,
And the other will disappear.
Then make an intelligent, organized kick,
Get rid of the weights that crush.
Don't worry about the bum on the rods,
Get rid of the bum on the plush."

He stopped. "That's all." He got off his chair without any help. He pulled a dirty piece of rag out of his pocket and carefully brushed his chair off with it. He sat down. He didn't say anything for a while, just sat and stared straight ahead of him. Then, still staring straight ahead, he said, "Well, that's the way it was. That's just the way it was. That's the kind of poems I recited in my organization, telling the bosses off."

The wide appeal of the IWW in the early 1900's can best be understood through men like Rickety Stan, what they were, what they saw themselves as, what they perceived they might have been, and, more important, what other people thought they were. Living though they did in a world of their own, they still knew how they were regarded by the larger world outside. And the knowing grieved them. They always tried to hide their grief. The sad old ones alive to tell the tale still try to hide it. But they seldom succeed.

Rickety said, "I was a lone wolf all the time. I never cared nothing about what them crazy scissor-bills or townies thought of me. They didn't think I was good enough. I didn't think they was either." He said that in one breath. In the next one he said, "Nobody knows how a man feels to get treated like a dog and to have nobody care if he lives or dies. I came in a town and I seen the way everbody looked at me like I didn't amount to nothing. Just because I was shabby. One time I went to church in some town. I don't know why I done it. All of a sudden I just felt like being in a church. So I walked in one. I kept praying to God that He wouldn't let nobody in that church hurt my feelings."

"Did anybody?" I asked.

Rickety said, "Yup." He started to laugh. "My union used to sing songs about what hypocrites church people was. You want to hear one?"

I said, "Sure."

Rickety said, "The name of my song's 'Long Haired Preachers Come Out Every Night.'"

"Long haired preachers come out every night," he sang,
"Try to tell you what's wrong and what's right,
But when asked how 'bout something to eat,
They will answer in voices so sweet:

"'You will eat by and by,
In that glorious land above the sky,
Work and pray, live on hay,
You'll get pie in the sky when you die.'

"And the starvation army, they play,
And they sing and they clap and they pray,
Till they get all your coin on the drum,
Then they'll tell you when you're on the bum.

"You will eat by and by,
In that glorious land above the sky
Work and pray, live on hay
You'll get pie in the sky when you die.

"Workingmen of all countries unite,
Side by side we for freedom will fight.
When the world and its wealth we have gained,
To the grafters we'll sing this refrain:

"'You will eat by and by
When you've learned how to cook and to fry:
Chop some wood, 'twill do you good,
And you will eat in the sweet by and by.'"

After he finished his song Rickety fell exhausted into his chair, but he was triumphant. "That's some fighting song," he said.

I said, "Yes."

"You sing a song like that," he said, "you can't feel like a bum no more." He smiled at me. "Jeez, thanks."

"For what?" I asked.

He said, "For helping me to remember. You should have heard us singing with all our voices together. Sometimes we used to put our arms around each other. We always sang about what us workers would do to the bosses and their tools. It was good."

The greatest appeal the IWW held for migratory workers lay in its anti-evolutionary approach and its preachments of struggle and revolt, its concept that down-and-outers must fight the employing class to the death. The preamble of its constitution makes this amply clear.

"The working class and the employing class have nothing in common. There can be no peace so long as hunger and want are found among millions of the working people and the few who make up the employing class have all the good things of life.

"Between these two classes a struggle must go on until the workers of the world organize as a class, take possession of the earth and machinery of production and abolish the wage system."

The IWW made the plain migratory worker a vital part of its strategy. Loyal members never were mere onlookers who had to accept the leaders' plans. They were functioning agitators assigned to harass employers and to create discontent until employers caught on to them and dismissed them from their jobs.

Rickety says, "I used to go on a job and meet my brothers there. They'd slap me on the back. 'Hey, Rickety! Hey Rickety, how long you think you going to stay on this job anyways?' I said, 'Well, maybe one week or two.' They laughed like hell. They said, 'One day or two would be more like it. Kind of good agitating you do, you'll get kicked out in much less'n a week.'"

I said, "What kind of agitating did you do, Rickety?"

"Well," Rickety said, "I'll give you a example. I'd get down to a berry camp, say, and start working just like I was a nobody and never heard of my organization. I acted innocent and I started talking to other fellows didn't belong to no organization and didn't know about the working class philosophy. I let them have it straight. I said, 'How do you like living the way you live anyways?' The fellows'd always say the same things I used to before my organization came. 'What do you mean how I like it? All I know I got to *live*. Right?' So then I'd say, 'Well, my friend, there's living and there's living. Why should bosses live so good and you and me live so lousy? Who says the world's got to be like that?' That's how I used to talk to hobos was working alone.

"I talked different to fellows had their women and kids with them. I used to tell them, 'Go on and look around at the boss's kids. You think they're dying from the t.b. or the big belly? Say, you got any idea when your kid's going to

come down with the big belly?' Sometimes I said something like 'Tell me something Joe or Steve or whatever the
name of the fellow I was talking to happened to be, when's
the last time your kid got a piece of candy?' Fellows with
kids always felt rotten when I asked them that. I used to
say, 'You know I was thinking of your kids a couple of
hours ago. I passed by the boss's house and I seen his kids
feeding dogs out of a nice box of candy. I seen them do
that three, four times. I started in thinking about your kids
and getting mad, so when I seen the boss's wife come out
waving her tail I told her, "You think this is fair? Here's
your kids giving candy to dogs and there's kids in your
own camps never tasted candy since the day they was
born." You know what she done? She petted that dog her
kids'd been feeding and she told me, "What do you expect
me to do about the kids in your camp? But these here
dogs," she says, "they belong to me and I got to take care
of them."' That's what I used to tell to Joe or Steve or
whoever."

I said, "Did that ever happen in a camp?"

He smiled. "Not exactly. I made it up to make fellows
mad."

As a preliminary agitator, Rickety Stan considered his
IWW missions finished only after he'd started a disturb-
ance among the employees and been discharged from the
job he was working. He was generally followed by other
agitators who utilized the groundwork he had begun and
went on fanning the discontent. These men were also fired.
The real organizers came in after they left. They were

smoother and more devious than the preliminary organizers. They worked cooly and quietly, so that employers seldom learned of their presence until after organization had been achieved and strike tactics been contemplated. Then they issued ultimata and made demands.

"Them bosses didn't know a real organizer when they fell over him," Rickety said, "but they was sure scared of little agitators like me. I remember one strike we had out in the hop fields in California. Wow! We burned down kilns, stuff like that. Guy by the name of Jack Slack organized it. None of the bosses knew he was the one. They all thought I was. A sheriff's man came with a whip and hit me over the face and punched me in the belly and threw me in jail."

"How long did you stay in jail?" I asked.

"Oh, a couple of weeks."

"What did you do after you got out?"

"Got me a different job."

"Was it a job you wanted to work, or did you go there to agitate?"

He said, "I went to agitate."

"What happened to you on that job?" I asked.

"I got beat up," he said matter-of-factly, "and threw in jail again."

"Then what?"

"I got another job."

"To agitate on?"

"Hell, sure."

I said, "Didn't you ever think of quitting your agitating, Rickety?"

"I couldn't ever have quit," he said. "What did beatings or jail matter compared to the class struggle?"

The IWW gave the old-time hobos roots. It gave them a chance to fight the system that they felt had deprived them of the ability to satisfy their normal drives for wives and families and homes of their own.

"Sure I was glad when my union brothers and I could scare the pants off of our bosses," seventy-one-year-old Big Belly Johnson, whose bare stomach protruded over the edge of his too-tight blue jeans, told me over lunch at Braemar's on the Bowery. "Why wouldn't I be? I used to be a married man and I lost my wife. Them capitalist bosses took her away if you want to know."

I said, "What do you mean, took her away?"

He said, "I mean they made a stinker out of her. She was sweet when we was married but she turned in to be a witch by the time I walked out on her. I could never get a job would pay me enough money to take care of her, so she had to work too. I was sorry about that but what could I do? I did my best for her, I was always so tired when I came home. O.K. So she was tired too. I never said she wasn't. But what could I *do* about it? I used to ask her all the time. She never had a answer. All she had was beefs and more beefs. She used to tell me, 'Why don't you do what other men do? Get out 'n' get me some money. What do you think I want to work all the time? I want to stay home and clean and cook for my man, maybe have a kid

191

or something. That's what I'd be doing too if you was a real man.'

"She had the nerve to tell me that. I asked her what she thought I was, a woman? She didn't answer me. So I said to her, 'What the hell you trying to do anyways? Make me feel bad?' She said, 'Ash!' That's all. She used to make me feel so bad. I don't know. She used to say she loved me. Some love. Soon as things got tough, where was all her great love at? I thought if she couldn't stick by me just because I was poor, then the hell with her. I figured if she hated me so much what was I sticking around her for? I thought I'd get out of town, find a good job and send her all the money I made. I thought if I could send her some money she'd start liking me again and then she'd act nice when I saw her so's I could start in liking her again."

When he used the word "liking," he really meant enjoying his sex life. He said that when he'd first married his wife, she'd seemed the most attractive woman in the world to him, but that after their disagreements had become intense he'd lain in bed with her and known that he ought to make love to her and still been unable to do anything.

"Sometimes I pushed her away. She used to turn over and start crying. I didn't care. I said to myself 'Good! Good! Let her cry!'"

But there were times when his wife didn't cry but laughed at him instead and called him unmanly.

Many old-time hobos know what Big Belly is talking about from their own experience. They tried marriage too and could not succeed at it because of the economics of their situations. Some walked out altogether, like Big Belly did, and wanted no more of sex and women once they'd given up their wives. But there were more like Don Juan Cinelli who still wanted other women after he left his wife and took them wherever and however he happened to find them.

"The more the merrier," he said in a cracked voice and winked his eye in an attempt to look gay and sophisticated despite his seventy-nine years and enfeebled little body. "I used to take 'em all, tall ones, short ones, fat and skinny ones. I believed in the old saying that all of them are alike in the dark. One girl's like any other girl."

I said, "Didn't you ever want a woman who would be just yours?"

At first he denied that he'd cared about whether his women had been promiscuous. He said he could have had any woman he wanted on any level he wanted her, from marriage right on down the line. Why he had had one woman, the wife of one of his bosses on a construction job he'd used to work, a real beaut, gorgeous legs, bosoms to make a guy cry, and she used to throw herself at him. Then there'd been the daughter of a farmer he'd used to work for. She'd been only a kid, a little over sixteen. She'd been inclined to embarrass him with her passion.

And then one day after I'd known him for some four months he told me that there were three girls he'd met in his life who could have meant something to him. He guessed he could have fallen in love with any of them.

Could have but didn't. Because what was the use of a man like he'd been falling in love? It took more money and steadier wages than he had ever earned to enable a man to make a life with a girl.

Most of the old-time hobos I met were thwarted men who might never have begun to wander, had it not been for the economic insecurity which broke up their lives. They had all of the normal instincts but no opportunity for gratifying them. And they resented their lack of opportunity. That is why the concept and program of the IWW was a godsend to the great mass of them. It gave them a vent for the resentment and helped repair their battered egos.

"I was the bravest striker you ever saw," Big Belly Johnson said. "If orders came to burn down a building I'd do it easy."

"How did you feel when you burned down buildings or participated in strikes?" I asked.

He said, "Wonderful."

I asked, "Why?"

"I don't know exactly," he said, "unless maybe it was because I didn't see myself as a leaf in the wind when I was striking. I always wished my wife could see me."

"Why did you wish that?" I asked.

"Because then she'd have to know what I was. She wouldn't think I was a nothing any more. She'd know I was a man."

Schloime the Troime smiled when I told him what Big Belly had told me. "A man," he said, "that's right. By me a organization what's able to make a poor fellow feel so good like the big union made Big Belly it's something to be very proud, no? Believe me, it's something to make a man what belonged to it he should hold his head up high. Like I'm doing now. The only thing I'm so sorry and ashamed, us members let our big union die. Now it ain't no more and you know what, us hobos ain't no more neither. Oy, it's very sad. I got a big pain by mine heart when I start in thinking. You know what is the hobo movement today? A nothing! A fighting between a bunch of characters they claim to be kings of the hobos. And also womens say they're queens. So what difference who is kings and queens of the hobos? They got something to do, these kings and queens? I'm telling you they don't got nothing to do." He smiled. "Maybe mine talk sounds bad to you, ha? It ain't nice a man should make such talk from his friends, but they don't deserve no better. By me, I don't talk bad because I'm jealous. Honest."

I said, "I know that, Schloime."

He said, "Kings and queens! Hoo, ha! And what makes me mad is that years ago some of these here men fighting they should become kings used to be a big part from the workers' struggle. Take mine friend Jeffie Davis. He used to be very important. All the time worried about the class struggle. But not lately. Lately, all he been interested was his picture should get put in the paper and everybody should say he's a king. A very big thing.

"He was a fine fellow, though, used to be king from the hobos when there was plenty hobos he should be king

195

from. He helped form a union, the International Itinerant Migratory Workers Union. That was 1908. But he ain't done so much since then except to try becoming a king."

"Did he become a king?" I asked.

"Yeah," Schloime said, "a couple times. Even though a couple hobos didn't used to like him so good."

"Why didn't they?" I asked.

"Because he picked himself up one time and he got married with a woman," Schloime said. "By me, myself, was nothing wrong with that, but plenty other hobos didn't like it so good. You know how it was. Us hobos used to say, 'A good hobo should stay away from women!' I never seen Jeffie's wife. He married with her in Cincinnati. That was where he used to be most of the time for taking care all the business by the union. One time he brung this woman to New York. All the hobos was mad then. They say he brung her in a car."

I asked, "When was that, Schloime?"

He said, "Nineteen hundred thirty, 1931. I can't tell you exact. And I shouldn't say about he brung her in the car exact neither. After all, I didn't seen him do it with mine own eyes. I only got it by other hobos. I don't like to believe it really happened."

I said, "Why, Schloime?"

He said, "You ask me why. All right, I tell you. A real hobo shouldn't be so weak he should be traveling in a car like he was a capitalist maybe. By me is hard to believe Jeff really done that. If yes, I think was his woman responsible. Maybe it ain't fair I should say such a thing like that,

I never seen this woman but, still and all, a man like my friend Jeff, just like that, he wouldn't travel in a car. Believe me, I told that to Happy Dan O'Brien too. He was the one first told me about Jeff's car. I told him 'Dan, that ain't such a nice thing you should say it without watching who you say it to.' But Happy Dan didn't care. He was a very nice fellow, only him and Jeffie used to always fight together."

"Why did they?" I asked.

"Well, because they was both kings I guess," Schloime the Troime said. "Being a king don't come so easy, you see. Jeffie, he got a lot of men on his side say he's the only king. By Happy is the same. There's others always wanted to be kings too, and by them they got men also say they're the only ones is kings of the hobos. You ever heard from Joseph Leon Cohen Segal Lazarowitz from Milwaukee, Wisconsin? That man, all the time he used to be a candidate for king. Also Jolly Joe Hamilton and Dr. Ben Reitman, a very smart man from Chicago. All these men was mine friends back in the good days. Not that they wasn't trying to be kings then too. I would be telling a lie if I said no. Only then they used to have worry from other things also. Now they have worry from one thing only. They should become kings and get their pictures in the papers.

"In the good days, us hobos got together for meetings we should talk over how we could make the workers' lives they should be a little easier. All right, so we voted for kings too. A little comic with all the serious. But now is no more serious. Is only comic. Every year is a hobo convention in Britt, Iowa. Hoo, ha. Some convention with nothing happening only kings and queens gets elected there. No talk from workers no more. All kinds people comes to Britt and stares on the hobos like they was the fat ladies from the circus."

"Then why do the hobos go to the meetings?" I asked.

He said, "Poor little people. Is nothing better to do. Also Britt gives away mulligan stews to them for free. So they go to conventions and make a parade all the people in Britt should make fun from them and then they elect a king."

"Why do hobos want to be kings?" I asked.

"Why?" Schloime answered. "Why? Who knows why? Maybe because when they become kings and get their pictures put in the papers, they forget how poor and sad they're living. Also while they make up tricks is going to help elect them kings, maybe they think they are very smart men."

"What kinds of tricks do they make up?" I asked.

"All kinds tricks," he smiled. "Take Jeffie Davis. One time he took in new members by his organization. Charley Chaplin. Al Jolson. Walter Winchell. All the time he took in a new member, he got his picture put in the paper. Dumb he was not. But his brains was used for wrong things.

"Then there's Benny Benson. He been elected a couple times he should be king of the hobos. He got brains too. So what he does with them? I tell you what. All he does, he sits around, makes up tricks he should get *his* picture in the paper more times than Jeffie gets his. A couple years ago he wrote some letters to a New York paper goes by the name the *Daily News*. He says in his letter that he is a very popular fellow by the hobos and everybody loves him and four times already he been elected king from the hobos. So he says New Yorkers should vote for him he should be mayor from the city and he writes in a platform—by all Americans they shouldn't have to work only four hours a day, four days a week, and they should also get three months' vacation a year. Nu, so what he does by the platform is get his name in the paper, people should only die from laughing at the hobos.

"Is sad, I'm telling you, very, very sad. This is what's become from the fighting hobos of the IWW. Is nothing left from that spirit. Why not? I tell you why. Because is the hobo's life today the kind of a life makes him feel he's a nothing. Because is nothing left from the IWW spirit used to tell hobos: 'First of all, you got to know you're a man by you yourself.' Now is a spirit, 'You ain't no man. You're a bum.'"

8. Down So Low

Self-respect is a vanished commodity among Skid Row-ers, U.S.A. The philosophy of the old-time hobo who conceived himself as a member of the wide working class rather than a lone failure has no semblance of reality today. And the IWW, "the one big union," which, having been conceived and nurtured along the Row, offered dignity in identification, is basically ineffectual. There are no proud Skid Rowers today, and there is no "one big union," to elicit pride. There is only a vast mass of egoless and handicapped people, and there are a very few movements consciously designed to "lift them up."

But the uplift movements along Skid Row today have been organized by outsiders, not Rowers. They have worked somewhat condescendingly, despite the best intentions of their administrators, and have been unable to achieve true identification with appreciable numbers of Skid Row residents. All of them have, in the last analysis, limited their operations according to their motivations.

The many missions along Skid Row, U.S.A., are there

primarily to "save souls for Jesus." Whatever help they give Rowers as people is aimed around their prime purpose. And the few municipal projects that have been set up are undeniably motivated by the needs of the general urban population upon whom unreformed Rowers are impinging, rather than by the needs of the people they are attempting to reach.

Alcoholics Anonymous is the only organization aside from the missions and municipal agencies which is attempting to work along Skid Row. But Skid Rowers are not the prime concerns of Alcoholics Anonymous either. That organization was set up to reach alcoholics, not Skid Row drinkers, and there is a vast difference between the two types. As a matter of fact, AA's most effective work to date has been among alcoholics who have not yet hit Skid Row. The only Skid Rowers who have been helped to any appreciable degree have been some among the small minority who have been driven to the Row by their whisky addictions and hardly any among the vast majority of egoless men. Still the program must be listed as among the most effective of the rehabilitative efforts along Skid Row today.

Alcoholics Anonymous is a group of ex-alcoholics who have banded together to help themselves keep sober by helping others to escape their compulsions. They maintain more than four thousand local clubs all over this country and have well over one hundred fifty thousand members. They hold group meetings in ninety-five prisons *and are accorded visitors' privileges in many hospitals that cater to alcoholics.*

Maria Donegan is an ex-drunk who doubtless would never have left the Bowery if it hadn't been for her contact with AA. She is a tall, well-formed, attractive woman in her mid-forties. She has gray-green eyes and hair that has gone prematurely white.

I first met Maria in the colorful, comfortably furnished Riverside Drive apartment she shares in New York with another AA'er, a woman of her own age named Rena Sachs.

"I lived on the Bowery for seven years on and off," Maria said. "I don't think I ever drew a sober breath in that time. Now it seems like a nightmare. But I don't want to forget how I was. I mustn't allow myself to forget. I have to keep telling myself what I am, a drunk, not an ex-drunk. I know as well as I know that I'm sitting here that if I had one drink with you now I would be unable to stop. It may not seem so to you, but right this minute I am only a short distance from the Bowery flops."

Maria Donegan was the only child of wealthy parents who adored her and indulged her every whim.

"I had everything I could possibly want when I was a young girl," she said. "To be truthful, I had more than I could want. I don't think I ever had to express a wish for anything material, because Mother and Dad both made a point of trying to predict my wishes. They were never very fond of each other and so they were always competing for my love. They began from the day I was born and I guess they'd still be doing it if I hadn't shamed them after I became an open drunk.

"I say an open drunk because I'd been a drinker for many years before I hit the Bowery. I began drinking heavily before I was sixteen. I'd go to a party and get thoroughly liquored up and have to be carried home."

Maria married George Donegan when she was eighteen years old. He was a big bluff extrovert who loved parties. He drank heavily too.

"At that time I didn't know the difference between an alcoholic and a heavy drinker," Maria says. "Whenever George admonished me I'd tell him, 'Women are out of the dark ages now. What's sauce for the goose is sauce for the gander.' When he told me that he had his drinking under control and could stop any time he really wanted to, I told him I could do the same. A small voice in me said I couldn't, but I beat it down. Whenever I got liquored up I started feeling sorry for myself, and so I had to keep on drinking until I drowned the sorrow by passing out. I think George used to wait for me to pass out, because he was always fearful I'd make scenes. I did make terrible scenes at parties."

"What about?" I asked.

She said, "George mostly. I always accused him of being unfaithful. He wasn't in those days. But I accused him anyhow. He couldn't greet a woman pleasantly without my assuming he had either gone to bed with her or else was intending to."

Maria Donegan's only daughter, Maurine Elise, was born when Maria was twenty-two.

"She was a beautiful little girl," she says, "and I was very proud of her. But I was also jealous. I was so terribly spoiled, you see, that all the attention the baby got seemed stolen from me. I couldn't bear to have George look at her lovingly. I used to ask him why he couldn't look at me the way he looked at Maurine Elise. When he laughed I wanted to kill him. I was even jealous of the way my parents loved the baby. I was always asking my mother whether she loved Maurine better than me. I had terrible visions in which my baby took sick and died and George and my parents all banded together to accuse me of wanting her dead. I started drinking during the day. I'd begin right after breakfast when George left for work and go on until I passed out cold."

One night during the year Maurine Elise was five years old and Maria was twenty-seven, Maria set fire to her house. Fortunately, her next door neighbor saw the blaze and called the fire department before it spread.

After that incident, George took Maurine Elise and moved into an apartment and Maria went back to her parents' home. She was miserable there and went on with her solitary drinking.

"But Mother persuaded me to see a psychiatrist. I went the first time to do her a favor since she was so convinced he could help me. Of course I didn't think he could because I was absolutely certain I needed no help from anybody. I could stop drinking any time, but what was the use of stopping when my life was so dreadful? A husband who had left me and taken my child. When Maurine Elise was out of my life I could convince myself that I loved her and wanted her back. I saw the psychiatrist three hours a week for two years. After a while I went because I liked unburdening myself. The man offered a sympathetic ear. Sometimes after a session I could go without drinking for two or three days. Never any more.

"My psychiatrist suggested that Dad send me to the Blandon Sanitorium in Pennsylvania. It's a very lush place, more like a summer hotel than a hospital. They gave me all kinds of medication and there was a psychiatrist on regular call. I was supposed to have been deprived of liquor, naturally, but I discovered various sources for getting it. All the same, when I went home after eight months I had had some long, sober periods and was more than ever convinced that I was the master of my own destiny. I wrote a letter to Dad in which I described my progress, thanked him for what he had done, and begged him to do me one more favor.

"If you can persuade George and my child to come back to me," I wrote, "I can promise you that I will never have another drink as long as I live. Dear Dad, I depend upon you."

Maria doesn't know what tactics her father used, whether he threatened George or appealed to his conscience, but her husband came to drive her home from Blandon. He took her to his New York apartment.

"I didn't like the apartment," she says, "and hated the

housekeeper George had hired. Her name was Mrs. Belcher. She was a big woman with a red face and the most penetrating black eyes. She had a German accent. George had hired her right after he'd left me, and she'd had a free hand in running his house. She was very possessive about him and especially about Maurine Elise. Today I can admit that she adored the child, but then I thought she was putting on an act. Besides, I always thought she watched me like a hawk with the hope that I would fall off the wagon again."

Maria begged George to get rid of Mrs. Belcher. He wouldn't do it, and she became furious with him.

"I told him he was preventing me from making the complete recovery which the authorities at Blandon had said I could make. I said, 'Someday, George, you'll look in the mirror and hate yourself for what you're doing to me. I'll never stop drinking so long as that woman's around disapproving of me. No human being could. She sits around waiting, just waiting, for me to slip. I'd like to smash her face in. You're waiting for me to slip too. I hate you!'"

George was always very tolerant, and Maria was annoyed by the tolerance. She characterized it disrespect. She spent hours conceiving original ways for breaking him down, and she dreamed of all the good, sympathetic folk she'd known along Skid Row. They didn't disapprove of her. They didn't treat her like a recalcitrant child who had to be borne with gritted teeth. She belonged with them, outcasts though they were. This den of propriety presided over by George, the king dragon, and administered by Mrs. Belcher, the assistant dragon, was no place for her. Let George keep his housekeeper then. Him and his housekeeper and his daughter!

"Every time I thought of how George and Mrs. Belcher were misusing me I felt a desperate urge for a drink. I wanted to drown my sorrows. Whenever I thought about drinking, I thought about my friends on the Bowery. Skid Row Sadie and Pig Head Hattie and all the rest of them. They were human beings, not stuffed dolls who'd never known what it meant to suffer. Maybe they were just bums in the eyes of the world, but they were better for me than my own family had ever been."

One Monday after she'd been home from Blandon for about three months Maria Donegan went down to the Bowery and found Pig Head Hattie there. Pig Head happened to be in the money. She had a large bottle of sneaky pete, and she shared it with Maria. Then Maria sold her hat and scarf and stockings for seventy-five cents and treated Pig Head back. After they were through drinking, she invited Pig Head to the apartment for lunch.

"I tell you we were a sight when we walked into the building," she says.

The doorman looked shocked. So did the elevator man. He couldn't take his eyes off Pig Head and missed the seventh floor, Maria's stop. She upbraided him dignifiedly but strongly.

"These service people," she said to Pig Head, "should be better trained. Don't you think so, dear?"

Pig Head laughed.

Maria said, "They really should though, dear."

She rang the doorbell forcefully. Mrs. Belcher came running. "What is?" she asked in a half-hysterical voice. "What is, ha? Tell me what is."

Maria put her arm around Pig Head's shoulder and patted her reassuringly.

"Pig Head dear," she said, "our servant wishes to know what is. Shall we tell her?"

Pig Head said, "Aw, hell."

"Spoken like a true friend and a gentlewoman," Maria said. She pushed in front of the housekeeper and dragged Pig Head into the apartment with her.

"Shall we retire to the living room?" she said. Then she turned to Mrs. Belcher. "Luncheon will be at one o'clock, as usual."

Mrs. Belcher asked, "Where, ha?"

"In the dining room, where else?" Maria said. She was delighted with herself because she had managed to confuse the housekeeper this time.

Her satisfaction was short-lived though. Before she and Pig Head had been in the living room half an hour, George came in.

"Well," Maria said, "fancy meeting you here."

George said nothing.

Pig Head laughed.

Maria said, "Now that you're here I suppose you'd like to have lunch with us. I shall ask Mrs. Belcher to set another plate."

"You must be losing your mind for real this time," George said.

Maria didn't deign to make any reply. She just changed the subject. "I presume your beloved spy Belcher phoned to let you know I was entertaining and you came to see for yourself."

George said, "I want her out of this apartment, Maria," pointing a finger at Pig Head Hattie.

Pig Head said, "You better not do nothing like that no more, big boy. I could bite your little finger off your hand and chew it up for horse meat."

Maria said, "Please treat my guests respectfully, George Donegan. If you don't I'll go down to the Bowery again."

George put his head on his hand. "Go," he said, "go."

Pig Head started to laugh again. "I'll go with her then," she said. "You'll feel awful bad to lose me, won't you? Don't say no because I won't believe it." She went to him and chucked him under the chin.

He looked as if he wanted to hit her; Maria recollects today.

"Yes, go on," Maria said, "*hit* a lady and a friend. I dare you."

Pig Head said, "I double dare you. I'll break your head open and call the cops if you hit me."

Today, Maria Donegan is deeply ashamed of how she baited her husband.

"I could die whenever I think of that poor man and the paces Pig Head and I put him through," she says. "He hung around all afternoon. I guess he was afraid to leave us. Or maybe he felt forced to torture himself and see how really low I could get. I made him get Mrs. Belcher to serve us lunch, by the way. It was just terrible. Unfortunately for my later peace of mind, I was not too drunk to know what was going on. The recollections I have! Well! Have you ever eaten a meal with Pig Head? Then you know that knives and forks are foreign instruments to her. She kept using her fork to flatten her food and slush it all over her plate with. Every once in a while, she'd bend down to lick her plate. She'd say to George 'Hey, Fatso, can you do that?' She'd begun to call him Fatso sometime before we'd sat down to lunch. 'Hey, let me show you how, Fatso baby, hunh?' Then she'd get up from the table and come over to where George was sitting and try to push his face into his food. I remember how she and I screamed with laughter over how miserable he looked.

"Finally George got up from the table. Pig Head said, 'You better not go no place till Maria and me tell you O.K., Fatso. What I mean you better look out because if you don't I'm going to tell all the people you was trying to make monkey business with me!'

"George got a nauseous look on his face. He said, 'This is the limit, Maria. A man knows when he can't take any more.' I said, 'What do you want me to do, go back down to the Bowery?' He said, 'For all I care, you can go to hell.'"

After George left, Maria and Pig Head ransacked the apartment for salable, transportable items. They took shoes and dresses and a fur coat and brought them to a pawnbroker named Nathanson. He paid them thirty-five dollars for everything.

"As you can well imagine," Maria tells today, "thirty-five dollars bought a lot of sneaky pete. I remember the beginning of our spree, though I can't remember the end to save my life. Pig Head and I began drinking in every dive along Third Avenue. We tried to pick young men up but they all steered away from us. Of course we landed on the Bowery. I met a young sailor there. I told him I was desperate for a young man and that I had money and more where that had come from. Nobody can know the depths to which we people can sink. The sailor let me take a room and came to it with me. I don't remember anything about him except that he was big and clumsy and kept saying, 'I can give you some party.' I can't tell you how long I stayed with him. All I know is that by the time I came to myself again I was in the violent ward at Bellevue."

During her time at Bellevue, Rena Sachs, her present apartment-mate came to see her for AA.

"How are you feeling now?" she asked.

Maria said, "What do you care how I feel? I wish I was dead and buried. Not that it's any concern of yours though."

"God help me," Rena said, "I know exactly how you feel."

Maria focused her eyes on the ceiling. "You couldn't possibly."

Rena smiled, "I was in this hospital plenty of times myself. In after one binge. Out again. Another binge. In again. I used to be a standing joke in the admitting office. One clerk always made special fun of me. He was a nice little fellow with a crew cut and a blond mustache. I wonder if he's still around."

Maria took her eyes off the ceiling and looked Rena Sachs over.

"You know, Maria," Rena said, "one time I ran into the street naked while I was drunk. My two children saw me. I had to wake up and face myself then. No more excuses. I had to admit I was a lush who had to stop drinking and couldn't hope to do it. I told my husband to take the children away because I wasn't fit to be a mother."

"Did your husband leave you?" Maria asked, in spite of herself.

"He left me all right," Rena said. "He'd had a bellyful of me."

"I'm sorry," Maria said.

Rena said, "Yes!"

"But why are you telling me?" Maria asked.

"So you'll know you're not the only drunk in the world," Rena said. "It's good to feel you don't stand alone at a time like this one you're going through. I know."

Maria raised herself up and waved her fist in Rena's face. "Don't you call me a drunk. I didn't ask you to come to see me. Believe me, I didn't need you. I can take care of myself. I don't need anybody to moralize over me, thank you."

Rena smiled, "I'm the last person in the world who can

afford to moralize over anybody else. I'm only here because I'm a drunk who has made the wonderful discovery
that I can stay sober myself when I help other drunks to
get well."

Maria Donegan was hard to get to. She was alternately
insulting and condescending. She was full of self-pity and
went on saying she was not a drunk either. But Rena
Sachs stayed with her for hours during the three days she
spent at Bellevue. And she finally managed to establish
a bridge of confidence with her. No nondrinker could ever
have hoped to do it.

First Rena reassured Maria, made her know over and
over again that she was in no sense unique. "Plenty of
us," she kept saying. "Oh, so many, Maria. Honest to
God." And then, when Maria still went on denying her
own alcoholism and blaming her drinking on circumstances, Rena was realistic and hardheaded with her.
There was not an excuse Maria could give, she told her
frankly, which she had not used herself at one time or
another. She pointed up holes in all of Maria's rationaliza-
tions and finally forced her to admit that she was an alcoholic.

Maria Donegan went home with Rena Sachs when she
was released from Bellevue.

"I can't begin to tell you what it meant to have her
ask me," she says today. "I told her, 'I've never been anything but trouble to anybody, and you hardly know me.
I could turn out to be a murderess or a thief. You'd be a
fool to risk taking me home.' Rena said, 'I don't think so.

I know you better than you think, you see. I know you because I know myself.' That touched me. But I went on giving her a hard time. I said, 'You ought to be spending your energy on somebody who can still be helped. I'm beyond help. I'm hopeless.' That's the way I was then, a mass of crazy contradictions. On the one hand I wouldn't admit I was a drunk, and on the other I said I was beyond help and hopeless. Rena was so wonderful though. She smiled at me and said, 'In AA we don't know what the word hopeless means. The only hopeless drunks we know are psychotics and people down with wet brain. We have a good story in AA about the word hopeless. A new member was talking to an old one about a poor drunk who had been on and off the wagon a hundred times. He said, 'I don't want to sound mean but I believe in being realistic. You've got to admit this fellow is hopeless.' The old member laughed. 'Hopeless?' he asked. 'Do you mean the son of a bitch isn't breathing any more?'"

Maria Donegan feels that the day she met Rena Sachs was the luckiest one in her life.

"I got myself talked out the first week after I left Bellevue," she says. "Rena and I stayed up till four or five o'clock every morning. She was a father confessor and a psychiatrist to me. I told her how I felt toward George and Maurine Elise. I was astonished by the truths that came pouring out of me. I felt wonderfully relieved after I was through talking. I can't describe the feeling. It's as though you'd been carrying an overwhelming burden one moment and then all of a sudden you'd been permitted to lay it down. I said, 'Rena, if only I'd had a confidante before I might never have become a lush.' She told me not to underrate my problem and said this first week was no test of anything. I discovered how right she was on my second week out when my craving for liquor seemed to have become more unendurable than it had ever been before. I was more nervous than I'd been. Sometimes my whole body shook and I had fits of perspiration. I'd have to change my bed sheets four or five times a night. Rena was wonderful. She stayed up with me every night I needed her to and took time off from the ad agency she works with, in order to be near me during the day. A mother couldn't have done more."

Rena began taking Maria to AA meetings soon after she left the hospital. She found them thrilling. At first she was drawn only by the companionship and the feeling that she was with her kind of people at last, but after she'd attended a few meetings she was also won over by the philosophy contained in "The Twelve Steps" by which AA'ers regulate their lives.

"AA's 'Twelve Steps' are full of good plain horse sense," she says. "First you have to admit that you're powerless over alcohol. Then you have to request help from a Higher Power, God as you understand Him. That phrase 'as you understand Him' is very important in AA. You may understand God differently from what I do, and I have no right to impose my way on you. An atheist may think of his inner self or even a radiator as his Higher Power. The way you see God is not important in AA. All that matters is that you learn to pray to Him for strength, although in your own way, of course. Then you must take a sort of personal inventory of yourself and resolve to make amends to people you have hurt. After that, you are ready to undertake the Twelfth Step and start trying to bring the AA message to other drunks."

Maria Donegan is a highly effective Twelfth Step worker. She spends a lot of her time contacting drunks in jails and hospitals and so naturally comes across many Skid Rowers. She took me to several meetings in New York. They were held all over the city in neighborhoods ranging from exclusive Park Avenue to the Bowery.

In AA, corporation presidents and stevedores, society matrons and domestics, doctors and bakers and taxicab drivers, Catholics and Protestants and Jews and Buddhists and agnostics and Communists and Republicans and Skid Row habitués meet harmoniously together. People who "really have the AA" are unique at first sight. Having fought their own difficult inner battles they feel a warmth and sympathy, not just a tolerance, for the people who are still fighting theirs. And they are desperately involved with one another. One member's victory is everybody's celebration. True AA'ers are members of their group first and individuals only second. All their activities are geared toward the recognition that each member is a small part of a great whole. Personal anonymity is really striven for in AA. True members refuse recognition for significant achievement and avoid having their names and pictures broadcast, filmed, or publicly printed.

"Why should we be publicized as individuals?" Maria Donegan asks. "What are we doing when we help sick drunks to recover? No more than what other drunks did for us. Paying back a debt if you want to put it like that."

One of the first AA meetings I ever attended was an interracial one in Harlem, New York. It was held in a Negro lodge headquarters, a barnlike room with California blue walls lined with Turkish tapestries and with red corduroy draperies on the windows. About sixty people sat on folding chairs. Perhaps fifty were Negroes. They ranged from well-dressed to Skid Row shabby. I tried to tell how many were former Rowers but found I couldn't. You never can draw conclusions from appearances at AA meetings. The attractive man with the white hair and the blue suit whom you might take to be a minister could have been in and out of jails from New York to San Francisco for all you know, and the fat, ungirdled female whose hair keeps falling into her eyes could be a first-time visitor like you are.

At the Harlem meeting I was mistaken for an alcoholic by a plump, dark-skinned woman named Rowena Ballast. She was sitting in the third row with her husband Marty when Maria Donegan and I arrived and had to push in front of her to take our seats.

Rowena smiled when I apologized for pushing. She had very white teeth. "It's O.K., sugar," she said, "the chairman's still giving out the glad hand. All he said so far is if he'd knowed there was going to be so many new faces here he'd have baked a cake. Funny thing is he's a baker by trade. His name's Kim Mack."

Kim Mack was a small, well-groomed man. His complexion was very dark. He wore a blue business suit, a white shirt, and a light gray tie. He smiled while he talked.

"Ladies and gentlemen, some people are able to get the AA program while they still have wives and families. But there are some of us who have to lose everything before we can realize where we stand. That's what made the saying that there are low-bottom drunks who lost everything and high-bottom drunks who still got a few things. If you're one of the high-bottom kinds yourself, don't get snooty and say 'This AA stuff ain't for me. It's only the guy in the gutter needs it bad.' If you think that a-way, remember what Bill W said. 'The difference between the high-bottom drunk and the low-bottom drunk is that both are laying smack in the gutter, but the high-bottom drunk has his head on the curb.' Bill W said that and he knew what he was talking about."

"Bill W's our founder," Maria Donegan whispered to me. "He's a terrific guy. He used to be on the New York Stock Exchange but he drank himself out of everything he earned. The idea of AA first occurred to him while he was in a lush hospital in 1933. In 1934 he contacted the man we call Dr. Bob in Akron, Ohio, a drunk too, and the two of them formed AA out of their mutual misery."

Kim Mack went on talking. "Maybe you think you're not a drunk. Maybe you think you're just a little bit alcoholic. Well, let me tell you, my friends, you can't be a little bit alcoholic no more than you can be a little bit pregnant. Think it over. We're all drunks. Join us if you think you're one."

Rowena Ballast put a tentative hand on my lap. "Look, sugar, do like Kim says and join us. Don't be afraid of nobody hurting you here. All any of us wants to do is help."

I said, "I'm not an alcoholic."

Rowena said, "Now, where'd I hear that before? Oh baby, all the times I used to say I wasn't one."

Maria said, "Mrs. Harris is writing a book, Rowena."

Rowena looked at me and then burst out laughing. "Well, bless your heart, sugar. I'm real glad you *ain't* one of us."

Kim Mack smiled at Rowena and me. "You two cooking up something the rest of us ought to know about?"

We both shook our heads no.

"Now," Kim said, "you new people's going to hear from five of our members. They all got different stories to tell, and we hope there's something in one of them will hit you where you live. If not, try to keep on coming to our meetings anyways. You never know when you'll hear some drunk's story that'll sound exactly like your own."

Marty Ballast, Rowena's husband as it happened, was the only one of the five speakers who had been rescued off Skid Row. He was a big, taffy-colored man in blue jeans and a red-and-white striped shirt. He looked to be in his late forties. He began his talks with the standard

AA line. "My name is Marty Ballast and I am an alcoholic." Not an ex-alcoholic. Not a recovered alcoholic. A plain alcoholic.

"I was down so low," Marty said, "I began drinking when I was fourteen years. Me and my daddy begun to get drunk together. I used to go out working them farms out of Richmond, Virginia, where we was living, and my daddy said if I could do a man's work on them farms there just wasn't no reason why I couldn't drink a man's share of whisky neither. My mama was a good churchgoer and she like to've cried her eyes out when she seen me guzzling whisky the first time. She begged me to quit and never do it no more. I promised her. But then she got sick. Daddy and me tried getting her in the beat-up old hospital they got for colored but there wasn't no room for her so she died. I begun to grieve real bad and the more I grieved the more I drunk.

"Daddy said now that Ma was dead and there was just him and me, us ought to get together and come up North. We come to New York. My daddy liked the big city but I was dead scared of it. So I kept on drinking whisky."

Marty Ballast was sixteen when he and his father hit the Bowery and seventeen when his father died of exposure one Saturday night.

"I went on thinking to myself I ought to get off the Bowery after Daddy died but I never done nothing. I just stayed and stayed and stayed."

"And drank and drank and drank," Rowena added with a laugh.

Marty patted her head. "Baby, you ain't joking," he said. "The life got in my blood after a while and I begun to think I wasn't never going to leave it."

"Me too, sugar," Rowena said.

"This here's Rowena," Marty told his audience. "She and I is married. I met her down the Bowery. She couldn't stop her drinking neither. She'd began it when she was twelve. Poor little old girl. Her ma was not respectable nor churchgoing, and she let men come to her house and get Rowena drunk."

Rowena and Marty Ballast, Bowery alcoholics for better than forty years, have been on AA for three years now. They have not taken a single drink in all that time.

"It's AA," Marty said, "not us."

Rowena said, "That's a good gospel, Marty. Come on and preach it loud this evening."

A man in the back row said, "Yes, yes."

A woman up front said, "Hear, hear."

"I come to AA in prison," Marty said. "I can't tell you how many times I been in and out, and it ain't done me no good. Rowena and me used to have a knock-knock joke about me and jail. It gone like this. 'Knock-knock. Who that? That's me. Who's me? Marty Ballast, don't you know? You again? Hell sure. When you going to quit coming here? When I die, boy, when I die.'"

"You quit before you died, sugar," Rowena said proudly.

Marty smiled and nodded at her. "This last time I been in jail a man worked there come in to my cell and told me to come on out and join a meeting some AA man was running. I said, 'What for? I am what I am and I don't dig none of this preacher stuff.' I came on out anyways just to get away from my old cell and I got real surprised by what I heard. This AA fellow was not no tub-thumper. No. No."

Rowena repeated, "No. No." So did a man in the audience.

Marty said, "He said good words."

Rowena said, "He touched my Marty where he lived."

Kim Mack said, "Hear. Hear."

Marty said, "That AA fellow seemed to be talking direct to me. He said, 'Give us a chance to help you.' I couldn't believe he meant me with my black skin and all. Later I asked him if he did and he said sure. I told him what did his society want old black folk like me in it for? He said a man's a man and his skin don't matter. I felt funny to hear that. I said, 'Only place I ever found where skin don't matter is on the Bowery.' He said, 'Ballast, how about you taking a chance on us? How about I send a AA man out here to visit you?'"

The AA man was named Larry Solomon and he came to jail three days after the AA meeting. He and Marty spoke for a long time. He said, "I want to come and pick you up when you get out of jail." Marty told him to suit himself. He never expected that he would really come, but he did. Not only that. He took him home to his own apartment and kept him there for a week. He kept talking AA to him.

When Marty left Larry's apartment for a furnished room and a job as a plumber's helper, Larry begged him to phone him any time of the day or night that he felt an overwhelming urge for a drink.

"Call me any time," he said. "You can reach me on the job daytimes. If I should happen to be out any night you need me, my answering service will know how to get in touch with me."

Marty Ballast had to call upon Larry many times. Once he called him at three o'clock in the morning. By the time Larry arrived at three-thirty he had downed most of a bottle of whisky. Another time he called him at six o'clock on a Sunday morning. He'd spent most of a miserable Saturday night trying to down his need for whisky. Larry came and stayed with him all day. They drank milk and talked until Marty grew drowsy.

"I wakened up about two o'clock in the afternoon," Marty says, "and Larry took me for a walk. He walked me right on in a big old Baptist church. I didn't want to go at first. I said, 'I ain't been in no place of worship since my mama died.' But Larry said to come on in because I didn't have nothing to lose. God come to me while I was in that church and told me to be a man and go on down the Bowery and get my wife and both of us to stop drinking from that day on. Larry and me went on down and got her and brung her back. Thanks be to God and all our AA friends we ain't gone on a drunk right up to this night I'm talking to you on."

It is no wonder that Rowena and Marty Ballast are unswerving AA'ers. All AA'ers are dedicated to their organization, but former Rowers who have really taken the program to heart are more dedicated than the rest. They live, breathe, eat, and sleep AA.

"AA keeps me and all the other low-bottom drunks like me alive," a former Chicago Rower named Albert Lee told me. "Of course we're dedicated. Dedicated as hell. So would you be. Say you were sick with cancer and one doctor in the world knew what to do to save you and spent all his time doing it. Wouldn't you be dedicated to him? Wouldn't you want to kiss his feet every day of your life?"

I met Albert Lee and three other AA'ers for lunch at their club in Chicago. Two of the men are lawyers. One is a doctor. Albert is in public relations. He is a tall man in his middle fifties with gray eyes and gray hair.

"I was the only one of the four of us ever hit the Row," he said.

The doctor said, "Don't boast, Al."

The two lawyers laughed.

Albert Lee said, "I had ninety-three jail sentences in New York, sixty-nine in Chicago, and twenty-three in Philadelphia."

"Why were you such a piker in Philadelphia?" one of the lawyers asked.

"Philadelphia always has made a piker out of me," Al answered good-humoredly. "Drunk or sober."

I said, "How long were you on Skid Row, Mr. Lee?"

"Twelve years," he said. "I began to drink in college

and went on drinking more and more heavily till I was in my middle thirties. My wife tried to protect me at first. But after I'd beat her up several hundred times she stopped trying and divorced me. My ego was hurt because, up until the day she left me, I'd fooled myself into believing that I was the one tolerating her. Everything seemed to blow up after she left. My boss who had put up with a lot of temperament and lack of dependability from me suddenly decided that he'd had enough. He offered me one more chance and I declined it grandly."

One of the lawyers said, "Grandiosely, you mean."

Albert Lee smiled. "I guess so," he said. "I made all the appropriate gestures. When he offered me discharge pay, I spat on the floor and told him to keep his dirty money.

"I didn't have to say it twice. I left my office for the last time with twenty dollars in my pocket. I drank it up that night. Then I went home and packed all my clothes and phoned the lawyer who was handling my wife's divorce action and woke him up out of a sound sleep. I told him I had just called to let him know that my wife could have our house and all the furniture as well as the few bonds we had managed to save. I was leaving town and all I intended taking with me were my clothes and some $870 in my own personal savings account. I saw myself as the noblest of fellows while I talked to him.

"After he hung up I called a cab and went to the Hotel Blackstone. The desk clerk wouldn't admit me and I became very rambunctious. I said, 'Every man's got to have a place to lay his weary head, for God's sake. If you won't let me into your hotel, at least suggest a place I can go.' He recommended the Gold Pheasant. That's how I came to hit the main stem."

At first Albert Lee was shocked to find himself on Skid Row. But it didn't take long for him to adjust.

"I was in a sopped-up state most of the time," he says. "I once tried to figure up the number of sober hours I had during all the years I spent on the stem. There couldn't have been more than sixty. I started out drinking whisky in the better places and ended up drinking sneaky on street corners or in the bloody buckets. I weighed ninety-nine pounds right before AA found me. A big man like me! I was a living skeleton."

Albert Lee joined a lush group when he first hit the stem.

"We were a sad-looking bunch all right," he says, "but we considered ourselves the aristocrats of Chicago. Our roster included such dignitaries as Benny the Bum, Stinky Lowery, and Pee Pee O'Donnel. We worked together to get our liquor, all for one and one for all. I found the living easy. Everybody thought I was a good fellow. I felt that they liked me; I liked them in return. For the first time in my life I had companions who didn't obligate me."

He stayed with his group for three years and then left by majority request.

"I would have had to have left a long time before," he said, "if the men hadn't been so tolerant of me. I constantly disobeyed the most important regulation of the group—that no member be unwilling to share his bottle with every other member. I couldn't bear to share mine. I used to try to fool my friends when I got whisky and make believe I wasn't holding out on them, but they knew damn well I was. I was really humiliated when they asked me to leave the group. I thought I must have sunk pretty low if these people could reject me."

After he was dismissed from his group, Albert Lee contacted his former boss and asked him to lend him carfare to Philadelphia.

"I figured I could grab hold of myself if I could just get to another city. Strangely enough, my boss was willing to let bygones be bygones and loan me the money."

Life in Philadelphia, however, was no different from what it had been in Chicago, except that now, with all his money gone, he had to panhandle for his sneaky and go to the missions for his food. He did odd jobs occasionally.

"I thought nostalgically about the happy companionship I'd had with my group in Chicago and so I tried to make contacts in Philadelphia," he said. "At first the boys would be delighted to have me but I was always asked to leave after they learned how sneaky I was about holding on to my own bottle. I was miserable without friends and managed to convince myself that I only drank because I was lonely. I got my first attack of the d.t.'s while I was in Philadelphia. And I was arrested twenty-three times as I told you before."

He thought a sojourn in New York might change his luck, but things were worse there.

"The cops kept an eye on me as a special character and I spent as much time in jail as I did out. I hated New York and kept longing for Chicago."

He hitchhiked from New York to Chicago. The trip took two months and a week.

"I looked up my old group the minute I hit the stem. I begged them to take me back but they wouldn't. I got hysterical. I remember getting down on my hands and knees and banging my head against the pavement. A couple of policemen came and took me away."

An AA'er came to prison to see him.

"He was young and handsome," he says, "full of buoyancy. I liked him at first sight. He came to see me often and picked me up the day I left prison. He carried me right off to a meeting. I considered it a wonderful experience. Everyone was so interested in me."

Albert Lee says that his experiences with Skid Row lush groups, unsatisfying as they were, predisposed him to make an adjustment in Alcoholics Anonymous.

"Of course I had to want to stop drinking before I could adjust anyplace. But wanting to stop wouldn't have been enough without the kindness and patience old members of my AA group showed me. You might say that AA represented the perfect transition between Skid Row and the world at large for me. AA didn't demand any more from me than my friends on the Row. As a matter of fact, they asked less, even while they were willing to give so much.

Nobody said, 'Man, you've got to stop drinking.' They only said, 'You've got to want to stop.'

"How different from my wife's world, my own before I hit the stem. There people would always be watching for my first failure. I don't mean they'd be hoping I'd slip. Nothing like that. I just think they wouldn't be able to believe that it would be possible for me to live without slipping. Then again, suppose I didn't start drinking again. They would never give me enough recognition. They couldn't know how much desperate discipline I'd had to exercise in order to avoid taking the first drink that would be bound to lead me on another binge. Only AA knows.

"Then too, there's the little business of needing to give for what you get if you're to keep your self-respect. If I had gone home to my wife, provided she'd wanted me, instead of to AA, I never could have had self-respect. Now I can go back but I couldn't have when I first came to AA. For in those days my wife and other people around me would have had to do all the giving and I, weak and scared as I was then, wouldn't have been able to give anything in return.

"But in AA I became a giving member of the group a couple of weeks after I came into it. My worst experiences could be put to beneficial use. I know how to reach other main stemmers who were as I had been. And, wonder of wonders, I could help them to do what was right in the world. Instead of helping them to get a bottle I could help them to give one up. That's a big job. I am proud to be part of it."

9. Jesus Loves Me

*There are about 1500 gospel or rescue missionaries along
Skid Row, U.S.A. They believe, as Alcoholics Anonymous
leaders do, that derelict Rowers cannot help themselves except through reliance on a Higher Power. They specify the
power as "the saving grace of Jesus Christ" and work to
provide Rowers with free beds and meals and washing facilities and clothes in His name. Some who have charge of
the larger missions claim to distribute as many as 400,000
free meals and to furnish as many as 65,000 free beds in a
typical year. And they say that, although the vast number
of men whom they contact use their missions for free flopping and eating, an appreciable number, as many as 800
a year, are brought to "new lives in Christ" through contact
with them and their institutions.*

*Scoffing Rowers call them "soul-savers" or Hallelujah
Boys, but they define themselves as "people who are sent
with good news to deliver those who need us from actual
or impending calamity." They have many living proofs of
their definition—people who had existed, before they met
the missionaries, without faith in God or man.*

Marty Stackett is such a living proof. He was converted nine years ago in a Chicago mission. He was about sixty when I met him, a palsied little man with a charming smile and a warm, sweet face. Before his conversion he'd had a feeling of estrangement from the world and felt guilty toward everyone he'd ever known intimately.

He traces his load of guilt back to when he was a little boy and lost his father. His mother had to work hard to support him and his three brothers. He remembers how much he wanted to help her and that he gave her trouble instead. When he was eight years old he did bad things to himself. His mother found him one night. She cried and said her heart was broken. She made him confess his sin to the priest, a young smooth-faced man named Father Muldooney. He cried, too, when he told what a bad boy he'd been, but he didn't stop sinning.

At sixteen there was a girl. He doesn't remember her name today. She and he used to be together under steps in hallways. He often wondered to himself how he could be so sinful as to go with her. But the wonder never stopped him.

When he was nineteen he fell in love. The girl's name was Jeanie. She was small and blond and beautiful. And he began feeling guilty about her from the moment she let him know she reciprocated his feeling. He thought he had no right to such a good, clean girl.

One day he told Jeanie about the other girl. He said, "She never meant anything, but I went on going with her anyways."

Jeanie said, "Look, Marty, was she pretty?"

Pretty? Well, she had been two years older than he, a fat girl with bulging breasts.

He said, "No, she wasn't pretty." She was ugly. In fact, the other boys around used to call her "pig." All the same, he'd bet they'd been in the hall with her too. He'd just bet they had. Dear God, all the time he used to spend wondering whether any of them had confessed her to Father Muldooney. He never had. He used to try every time he entered the confession box. He used to think, "Today I'll tell him." But the words wouldn't come. He wouldn't know what to say to the priest. How could he begin to tell Father Muldooney about the disgusting way he'd felt under the steps with that dirty girl? Like that first time when she had pulled him onto herself, his skinny body on her fat one, and the odor of her, dirt and sweat, and then he'd begun to feel himself sweating too. *Mea culpa,* Father Muldooney, I'm the lowest of the low. But he went with her again and again, all the same. He couldn't stop after the first time. Every time she asked him into the hallway he came. Sometimes he asked her. When she wouldn't go, oh, there were times when she did say no, he went home and locked himself in the bathroom. And he felt like the worst boy in the whole parish. He knew evil and sin were deep in him. Born and bred in sin, he would also die in it.

After he married Jeanie he forgot about the girl under the steps. But he had to learn to live with a new and worse sense of how sinful he was. For there were times when he behaved in the same way toward Jeanie as he had toward the girl under the steps. He grew hot and sweaty and lustful in bed so that his wife had to turn from him and vainly try to hold him off. She told him more than once that she was a pure woman and not an animal like that one he'd known before.

One evening, coming home from work, Marty thought of Jeanie and was suddenly overcome by the lustful feeling. He pictured himself coming in the door, grabbing her in his arms, kissing and fondling her until they both found themselves in the bedroom. So he didn't go home right after work. He went to Murphy's Bar. He drank himself sodden. That way he forgot his evil thoughts.

"Drinking used to help me forget how low I was," he says today, "so I kept on drinking more and more. I was terrible when I was drunk. I used to beat Jeanie up. Afterwards I'd go on my knees to her, but she got to hate me anyways. I didn't blame her when she left me. She should have done it before. She stuck it too long as it was."

"When did she leave you, Marty?" I asked.

"Nearly forty years ago."

About three months after Jeanie left him Marty hit the Bowery. For a while he worked odd jobs and lived in the better flops and ate in the better greasies. But his drinking was always done in the lowest dives he could find. And when he felt the shameful sexual stirrings, *mea culpa*, Father Muldooney, God forgive my dirty sin, why then he found the dirtiest fleabags in the neighborhood.

After a while, he quit going for the fleabags. His need for sneaky replaced his need for sex.

Marty had sixty-nine jail sentences in Chicago. Most times they kept him overnight, but there had been one time some eleven years after he'd hit the Row when they'd kept him in the workhouse for thirty days. He'd eaten and rested better in that month than he had in all the eleven years put together. Well, he'd thought when they'd released him, this is it, now I'll follow the straight and narrow. He'd gotten a job digging roadbeds, and although he continued to live on the main stem he had nothing to do with his old cronies. Till he met a man named Mike who said, "Look who's trying to get respectable." That set him thinking again. Mike was right to find him funny, a sinner like him. He needed to forget about Jeanie and how he'd abused her purity. He needed to put a load on.

During his twelfth year on the Row, Marty was hospitalized twice with the d.t.'s. That was the year he discovered that his shakes weren't necessarily connected with alcoholic binges. Sneaky or no sneaky, he had them for real and forever. His legs shook so much he couldn't walk on them. Drunk *or* sober. That was frightening. As long as he had sneaky though, he didn't need to think about it.

One night he fell down on the sidewalk and couldn't lift himself up. He made a few feeble attempts and then stopped trying.

Now he says, "That night my legs wouldn't carry me any more turned out to be my lucky night. My Savior was looking out for me. He saw to it I collapsed in front of the mission and Brother Johnny Johnson'd find me. I guess you'd say Brother Johnny wasn't much then, just a down-

and-outer like me. He worked around doing anything the superintendent wanted done. But he'd found Jesus. It showed right out in his face."

Brother Johnny dragged Marty into the mission and up to the second-floor men's dormitory. He placed him on a cot next to the one he slept on. He undressed him and then he brought water and soap and washed some of the deep-crusted dirt off Marty's body.

Marty was shocked to find himself in a bed when he wakened on the morning after. He looked around at the unfamiliar place, thinking with half his mind that he had the d.t.'s again, while he knew with the other half that d.t.'s never had begun this pleasantly. Still he found himself screaming just in case he did have the d.t.'s. Brother Johnny, who was busy cleaning the dormitory, heard him and came running. He was a big, burly, red-faced man.

"Hey, fella," he said with a smile.

Marty said, "Where am I, anyways?"

When Brother Johnny told him he tried to jump out of bed. "No Hallelujah house for me," he said meaningly. "I'm not that kind of guy."

"What kind of guy?" Brother Johnny asked. "Just take it easy, fella, that's all you need to do."

Marty didn't want to take it easy. There was something in him that wanted out of this place as desperately as he'd ever wanted anything.

Today he tells, "I don't know. I got cold shivers when I found out where I was. I figured myself to be the devil's child and I knew God's house was no place for me. I tried my best to get out of bed but I couldn't do it. My legs just wouldn't carry me. I got as far as the floor. Then I fell right down. Brother Johnny lifted me up and put me back in the bed. He was so nice. I said, 'What are you doing this for?' He said, 'I'm doing it for Jesus.' I started to cry. He said, 'You shouldn't be sad. You should be happy.' I asked him, 'Would you be happy if you were crippled? What'll I do now?' He told me not to worry. Jesus would take care of me. I remember thinking, 'He hasn't done it so good up till now. Why should He begin all of a sudden? But I kept my mouth shut.'"

Marty stayed on his cot for eight days. Brother Johnny and some of the other mission men brought him his meals. They washed him and kept his bed clean. They brought a doctor in to see him. The doctor gave him some pills to take and assured him that he would be all right. Marty didn't believe him. Whenever he found himself alone in the dormitory he cried like a baby.

One night Brother Johnny and another man begged Marty to come down to chapel with them. He didn't want to. But he couldn't see how he could logically get out of going. Good as they'd been to him, how could he say no to anything they suggested?

Brother Johnny lifted him out of bed, and he and the other man supported him down the stairs between them.

"You know," the other man said, "I used to be just like you. I was not able to walk. You should've seen me drag around. One night I dragged my legs up to the altar. When I say dragged, that's what I mean. I fell down twice. The second time I couldn't make it up so I crawled to the altar. Well, man, I didn't need to crawl away from it. After I finished praying I got right up and walked away on two feet."

Marty's first night at the chapel didn't mean much to him. When the superintendent spoke he listened politely and even attentively, as was fitting for a nonpaying invalid guest to do. When the men made their testimonials he tried to force his mind to accept the more miraculous ones and was happy for the men whose stories he really did believe.

After the first night he went regularly to chapel. And on his seventh night of attendance he had his own conversion experience. He still talks about it with profound emotion. He stumbles for words, fearful that any he chooses are too weak to express his feelings.

"I wish I could explain what came over me. The men were singing the song, 'Rescue the Perishing.' It goes, 'Rescue the perishing! Care for the dying, snatch them in pity from sin and the grave.' I thought of myself while I sang along. What was I if not one of the perishing? I must have been one like that from the day I was born. I never felt like I was a part of anything till that night at the mission when I felt Jesus's spirit right in me. I whispered, 'Please cure my leg and make me strong. I want to be a part of your world and I want to do good in it.' I had a feeling if God would only let me find Him, then I would find myself. I was so lost. I started to cry. I had to. There was a hurt in my heart. I knew I'd had it all the time but it was never so clear before why. Now I knew why I always felt like I did. Because my soul was conflicted."

He hesitates, but not for long. He wants you to know every wonderful thing that happened to him. "I was afraid to open my heart to God. I don't think I could have, except that here I was so miserable and I knew there was nothing else for me. So I opened my heart. When God came in He said, 'Now I'm with you. You need not be afraid of anything. Stop feeling so bad about the sins you committed. I am washing them all away.' Since then I haven't had a day of worry. I know my God will always care for me."

Marty's description of his conversion experience approximates that of almost every twice-born man I met on Skid Row. Their souls were tense before, they tell you, and now they feel calm inside. They are relaxed. Because they live with a consciousness of God they are no longer uncomfortable in their present lives or anxious about their future ones. Their fears are washed away.

A seventy-four-year-old man who looks twenty years younger, Howard Meredith, a pianist and singer at the world-famous *Christian Herald* Bowery Mission explains conversion this way.

"It's a feeling you have that you're right and you're square. You've got peace and content. You can go in a room and shut the door and sit down and you don't have to turn on the radio, you don't have to turn on the television. You don't have to do anything. You can just sit there. I can go upstairs and sit down by myself and I'm not embarrassed. I don't embarrass myself like I used to before I took Jesus as my personal Savior."

Howard Meredith came into the Bowery Mission when he was sixty-one.

"I'm very sorry to say that I was not exactly sober when I came," he said. "I staggered halfway down the aisle but I knew I had to get to that altar because I'd gotten to the place in my life where I was so terribly unhappy, too unhappy to go on living with myself. I used to get up in the morning and hate to look in the mirror. I had nothing to look forward to and I was ashamed to look back."

Howard Meredith, unlike the mass of mission converts, had never hit the Row in the true sense of the word. He was still living in his own apartment when he accepted Christ, a fancy apartment in exclusive Gramercy Park, and he had a good job managing a group of flophouses. But he drank as heavily as any of the Rowers who flopped in the houses he managed.

"I'd get a supply of liquor," he said, "and take it into the apartment and shut the door. I'd feel so miserable when I wanted to stop. I'd buy a bottle and set it on the mantel or someplace so I could see it and then I'd look but I wouldn't drink and then I'd pray to God to help me and promised him all sorts of things if he'd just get me over my horrible feelings. But stopping didn't help much. I knew I'd only start again. I always knew what booze meant to me—temporary suicide. When I drank, I stopped being Howard Meredith. I was no longer myself at all. I was somebody else and I didn't give a rap about anything. All

I had to do was to get a bottle and take three or four wallops out of it and then things wouldn't make any difference any more."

When Howard Meredith testifies at mission meetings, as he very often does, he is impressive. A small man with an assurance born of his salvation, he says:

"One thing I know, for the rest of my life I am going to tell someone else what Jesus did for me. The Lord often uses me in speaking to men at meetings here. Many a man in this neighborhood knows it. Men say, 'Tell me what you have that I want,' and they're on their knees to me. I have love for Jesus. Men know what I've got. They respect me for it. And it's all in this house I found it."

"This house" is located in the very heart of New York's Bowery. It is a clean, pleasant building, and its chapel, with lovely oak pews and stained glass windows, looks more like a cathedral than a rescue mission room. Its statistics are impressive.

Mission workers say they furnish 66,541 beds a year, serve 372,528 meals, permit 62,773 non-resident shaves, distribute 18,307 articles of clothing, and send 4,301 men out on jobs. About 5,350 men profess conversion annually, but when they are pressed to estimate how many souls they save they tell you that they don't know that because, "God keeps the real books."

Rev. George Bolton, director of the mission, says, "Our program is geared to bring conviction into the hearts of sinners. You could call us a "soul-saving" station. You could say that our motto is 'Soap, Soup, and Salvation.' Not that we ever force a man to claim to be saved just to get soup and soap. We'll feed him whether or not he comes to Jesus. And if he claims to come and doesn't really, we usually know that."

Mr. Bolton is in a good position for knowing when the men are sincere. He was an inveterate gambler before he accepted Christ as his personal Savior. By the time he wandered into Hell's Kitchen in New York, "to die there, I thought," his wife and children had left him and he felt he had nothing to live for any more. Today he is not only doing a superb rescue job on the Bowery, he is also an immediate past-president of the International Union of Gospel Missions.

"I was down," he says with deep emotion, "till I came to believe, honestly to believe, that this One called Jesus loved me enough so that he just died for me. Once I knew that I was born again. With God's help I was able to rise from the dirt, and then I was able to help others who were as I had been. Oh, it is truly gratifying to do that. Life is worth living, and no matter how much excitement I found before I came to Christ life wasn't very important. Now I thank God that He had me down before He lifted me. I wonder if good people who never had to be born again can understand how my heart glows—to have come from such a black abyss and now to be of service. I can't describe the feeling. Maybe another mission worker can tell you better what I mean. Ask them. Most of them were rolling stones like me and are twice-born men now."

Mr. Bolton is right. Most mission workers and especially

the most effective ones among them—there are a few rare exceptions among women workers—are men who were "sinners" before they found themselves in Christ.

Pastor Bolton's assistant, Raymond Allen, is one like that. He is a small man, bright with the stamp of success on him. When you see him rise to address his awkward, unwashed, shabby congregation you cannot help but be impressed with the dignity of his rising and the practicality of his speech for those whom he lives to reach. Like Pastor Bolton, he never talks down.

"I went through the school of hard knocks at a slow rate," he says. "I ran away and left a widowed mother and went off to see what makes this old world tick. It was all right at first. I didn't get into too much trouble. But you know you gain speed as you go along. Among the habits that became one of my pets was the old bottle. I got where I'd rather drink than do a lot of things, and I got where I had to do a lot of things in order to keep myself provided in drink."

He went into the insurance business during World War I and began to do well because money came and went easily in those days. But he drank up most of what he earned. Finally his reputation as a drinker caught up with him and he left the insurance business.

"I started a diner in the 1920's," he says, "when money was still plentiful, but the bartender in the speak-easy had a very good customer. And when the crash came after I was in business four years, I crashed right along with it. I cashed in my chips and started out to roam again this old world. But this time jobs was hard, food was scarce. It wasn't too many months until my clothes became ragged and I became very hungry, with no steady eating place. Something to think about, gentlemen, and I know that I feel for everyone of you who've ever been in business and then had it taken away from you because of your own work or because of neglect of some other kind. I realize what it means to be setting at the table one year and having things served to you and then the next year to have to go out and look under the lid of a garbage can for something to eat. I know what it means. I realize those awful days that you put in wondering just where the next meal was coming from."

As you listen to Raymond Allen you know that he is telling the truth. And as you look around at the people around you, you know beyond a doubt that they know it too.

"I knew nothing of missions in those days," he says, "knew nothing of what God could do for a man. But one day after putting in a few months of that running around and starvation coming upon me, I was in the city of Albany when a policeman chased me into a mission like this. You know you got to get pretty low when a cop'll chase you off the street, and that was exactly my position. Society didn't want me, no friends wanted me, nobody wanted me, and I didn't even begin to think there was any hope for me in the world of anything except this awful dragging your feet from one place to another, wearing dirty clothes, and always having an empty stomach. But I'm so glad for rescue missions, so glad to know that as a man chased me in there that day I heard something, and this one great word that I heard, that I didn't know, that I had been the biggest share of thirty-eight years learning, was 'Whosoever.'

"That may not sound too much to you tonight, my friends, but that afternoon as I sat there shivering in my sole possessions, the filthy rags that clothed my body, I heard one verse of Scripture that I didn't know was in the Bible—'Come unto me, all ye that labor and are heavy laden, and I will give you rest. Whosoever cometh unto me I will in no wise cast out.'

"I could see lots of reasons that afternoon for not coming. I could find lots of excuses for not obeying the verse that I heard, but I cannot tell you yet today what came upon me to the extent that I left my seat and why I found myself with a prayer; I cannot tell you yet to this day why I put those dirty fists heavenward and called upon God to do something for me. I had no use for God for all those years except to use His name in vain. But I'm glad for a God that understands. I'm glad for Someone who knows more about me than I know about myself. I'm glad for Someone who's big enough to take care of me when I can't take care of myself.

"And when I came to Him that day, an old penitent praying 'God be merciful to me a sinner, and save me for Jesus's sake,' He not only took the desire for drink out of my system but he put me upon my feet and put me to work. And today after twenty-two years, from the floor of a rescue mission where a newspaper served as a sheet, another one as a blanket, I am what I am tonight by the grace of God. The only reason I'm no more a drunkard is because Christ took the desire out of me. I couldn't quit."

Raymond Allen's congregation is always impressed by his testimony. You can see them at the mission night after night, waging their desperate inner battles and occasionally winning one and beginning the slow road to salvation.

Like that young man in his early twenties, dark-haired, dark-eyed, who suddenly sprang up from his seat one night when I was there. He grinned a toothless grin and sat down again.

Mr. Allen smiled at him. He said, "You got to find out the hard way that you can't help yourself by yourself. But God loves you enough to help you. I first heard that in a mission and I thought it was strange, God loving a filthy person like me. I didn't like looking under the garbage cans. I tried just as hard as you to get away from the life but I couldn't till God took me away. Fellows, it's not religion I'm talking about, it's a Person."

The toothless man rose again. He whispered, "Amen, A-a-a-men." Looking at him you got the feeling that he wanted to shout it to the skies, not whisper it the way he did.

A man beside him plucked his sleeve, trying to get him to sit down.

"A-a-men," he whispered once more before he sat.

"Tonight," Mr. Allen said loudly, "if I could just get you to see the picture of me in those days. If I could just get you to see it. I didn't belong to any church. That didn't make any difference. Jesus never says, 'What church are you in?' You're all the same to Him whether you come from Park Avenue or a park bench. Whether you come from Yale or you come from jail."

The toothless man nodded and clapped his hands.

Mr. Allen's voice grew gentle. "See," he said, "I was right where you men are today so I know you need more than what the Bowery Mission can give you. Sure, you'll get a stew. Sure you'll get a bed. But you need more. God'll give it to you. How do I know? I know because He did it for me. And I was dirtier than anybody here." He hesitated. "Fellows, this old world hasn't offered too much, has it? But you can look up. Come up to the altar now. Let's pray together. Take Jesus as your Savior. I beg you to come up and make a brand new contract with God. Come on up. You'll feel better after you take Jesus as your Savior."

The young man without teeth walked up. Mr. Allen put an arm around his shoulder. He brought him close to himself and held him there for a moment. Then the two of them knelt. Mr. Allen rose. The young man remained kneeling. An old, crippled, leprous-complexioned man came up. It was hard for him to kneel. Mr. Allen helped him. A white-haired, straight-backed man with a tear up his right pants leg came and disdained Mr. Allen's help. He kneeled by himself and looked haughtily upward.

Mr. Allen called for Hymn No. 179. The men bowed their heads and sang, "What a friend we have in Jesus, all our sins and griefs to bear."

Then, while the three penitents knelt, Mr. Allen asked

247

for testimonies from the saved ones in the mission. A few men gave testimony.

"I was drunk. I didn't want nothing but a handout when I drifted in this here mission. I took a long time before I seen God, thinking I was fooling Pastor Bolton and Mr. Allen. Well, I was the only one fooled. Because I didn't know it was God I was trying to fool. Thanks to Him, I found out. I ain't drunk nothing but water and milk for ten months. Me, a man who sold the gold out of my teeth to get money for sneaky. I wasn't able to break them chains. God done it. He was able."

"I was a coward. I used to run away. Every time I got in a little trouble I used to try to run away from it. I thought I was succeeding but now I know I wasn't. You can't run away. God won't let you. Tomorrow I'm going back to my family."

A small old man got up. "Thank God," he muttered tearfully, "for two days of salvation."

Mr. Allen went on preaching. "You gentlemen will never be able to escape God's invitation, 'Come.' That's all it takes. God doesn't want you to be smart or well-dressed or strong. All he asks is that you be heavy-laden. Sin and its consequences make the heaviest burden that anyone can carry. You've tried to fight your own battles. I know you've tried everything, you think. And yet here you are on the Bowery. You've tried the rest—now try the best! Try Jesus Christ! Believe me, He'll help you."

The men do believe Raymond Allen. They shuffle awkwardly forward, nine of them, ten, twelve. Fourteen men in all kneeled with Mr. Allen on a raw January night last year.

"Take them into Thy keeping," Mr. Allen prayed in behalf of those who had come. "Make them strong." There were tears in his eyes, and he made no attempt to hide them as he looked at the kneeling men. "Make them strong," he repeated. "Please make them strong." Then he prayed with each of the men individually. He wasn't finished until three o'clock in the morning. I knew he had to be awake at seven for a work project he was doing.

"I know what you're wondering," he said, smiling. "Where do we mission folk get the energy? We get it from God. He's given us a big job to do and He makes us equal to it. I thank Him for the energy and for the life He lets me lead. I thank Him for having put me in the gutter so I could get born right out of it and help Him help other men to do the same."

I told him I'd heard other missionaries talk the same way. He laughed. "Sure, we all talk alike. God lifted the others the way He did me. John Callahan used to talk like I do. He did a sweet job in the Calvary Mission right here in New York. He died a couple of years ago. So did Drunken Belle. She's dead too. She worked in Chinatown and at plenty of other missions around Los Angeles and San Francisco. She was a great big woman, a notorious underworld character who was always getting thrown out of saloons. Well, one time somebody told her about a mission where queer people sang hymns. She turned into a great mission worker. I guess if you'd heard her talk you'd have said she sounded like me.

"Then there was Steeple Jim Parker. Steeple Jim was a Providence, Rhode Island, man who'd been arrested there fifty times. One time he staggered into the Providence Mission with blood streaming down his face. People who saw him say God grabbed him up and threw him down prostrate at the altar. When he got up he began to preach and never stopped till he died. I find I say some of the things he said. It's lost sheep knowing how to talk to other lost ones.

"And last but not least, is Jerry McAuley. I think he was one of the greatest missionaries ever lived. He used to be a river rat before he got God. He'd go out with gangs and rob excursion boats. God came to him one night when he went out to rob a boat and slipped off it and almost fell overboard because he was so drunk. He came to him in a vision and said, 'Jerry, you've been saved for the last time. Go out on that river again and you'll never have another chance.'

"Jerry and his wife Maria opened the first mission in 1872. They took a room in an old wreck of a house near the Bowery and hung out a sign 'The Helping Hand for Men!' I guess I don't need to tell you Jerry never drank or river-ratted after that. In 1876 he moved his mission to a whole building on Water Street. It's still there today. He preached a great sermon the day he moved. One thing he said in his Irish accent I'll never forget. I been saying the same thing myself and I guess I'll go on saying it till my last breath.

" 'The way to help men is to set 'em to work. The minute they say they're sick o' the old ways, start 'em to pull in somebody else. You see when your soul is just on fire longin' to get at every wretch an' pull *him* into the fold, there's no time for your old tricks an' no wantin' to try 'em again.' "

Those, then, Jerry McAuley, John Callahan, Drunken Belle, Steeple Jim are the traditionalists of the twice-born missionaries. Like the present twice-born ones, they had an instinct for touching the hearts of the down-and-out, because they had once been down and out themselves. There are only a few of their sermons recorded today, but those which are show their approach to be exactly similar to the present-day one, never superior, never supercilious, always on a level for the people they want to touch.

Jerry McAuley's sermon illustrates how practical the early missionaries were. Later expressions are more elaborate but every bit as practical. And they all emphasize, as Jerry McAuley did, that an ability to empathize is the greatest gift a mission man can bring to his job. Considering themselves "soul winners" rather than teachers of doctrine, they are vitally concerned with the concept they characterize simply as "large hearts."

Dr. William A. Paul, a highly respected Milwaukee missionary and author of the *Rescue Mission Manual*, makes this point clearly.

"Our work must never become professional," he says. "If

the time ever comes when we can deal with men in sin and suffering without a heartache, without bearing their burden, we had better quietly get out of mission work."

Missionaries love the people they service, and their love is inherent in every message they preach. In the minds of mission workers, the Bible must have been written with their downtrodden charges in view.

"Take Matthew 11:28," Pastor Bolton says enthusiastically. "'Come unto me, all ye that labor and are heavy laden, and I will give you rest.' What could be a more appropriate text to preach to my boys? You can't think of one, can you? How about II Corinthians 5:17? 'Therefore if any man be in Christ, he is a new creature; old things are passed away; behold, all things are become new.' Isn't that passage wonderful? I've known it to help poor fellows who were down here because they always thought of themselves as low men whom God hated. When they understand II Corinthians 5:17, they know God loves them in spite of everything. And they become converted and lose their loads of guilt."

And converted men are happy men. They do not ever hesitate to tell you why. Many of them told me in missions all over the country. For some reason however, mainly its dedicated staff, I think, men from the Bowery Mission were able to tell me with greater insight into their own motivations than men from any of the other missions were. And so I quote some verbatim interviews from the Bowery Mission.

I talked to a tall, strikingly handsome, well-dressed man

in his middle forties. He was obviously a highly cultured man. He said that although he would be happy to talk for publication he preferred to maintain his anonymity.

"My name is legion," he said when I asked him who he was. "I could be any man out on that street tonight."

I said, "What were you doing before you came on to the Bowery?"

"I'd been in business," he said.

"What brought you here?" I asked him.

He smiled. "Just plain stupidity and a terrible ego. I thought I was a little too good for anybody including myself."

"What does the Bowery Mission mean to you?" I asked.

He stopped smiling. "Actually it means mental, physical, and spiritual peace. I learned to pray again in this place. I guess most of us think we're Christians. I was tired and I was hungry and I was lost, and I came in here realizing that saying you're a Christian and accepting Christ as a real person are two different things. In accepting Christ for what He's meant to be, I found I had forgotten how to pray in those churches on the outside because I had forgotten who He really is. He is a power greater than any one of us, and we must bow down to him. Since I've come to the Bowery Mission I've found a new prayer for myself. It has three lines so far. 'Thank the Lord for today. Be humble. Let Thy will, not mine, be done.'"

"Why is it," I asked, "that you learned to pray in this place above all others?"

"I don't know," he said. "That's something intangible,

something I can't put into words. You come in—now I'm certainly not competent to judge any man in this place— but you come in, you find a spirit and an innate courtesy —you hear the men, you see the men and there's a certain sincerity about them that it kind of makes me turn around and look at myself and not be very proud of me.

"You know Pastor Bolton and Mr. Allen took me in, asked me no questions, and gave me something to keep my mind occupied, which I needed more than anything. I guess if you ask for the thing I like most about the mission it's this —they're not interested in where you've been or who you've been but they hope to help you a little bit on what you're going to be."

The man who calls himself legion is one of the few people I met around mission circles who intends to leave "the life" eventually and to return to his former home. Of course he has no idea of when that will be.

"When you're a baby, you have to learn to crawl before you can walk. I'm now crawling and pretty soon I'll begin to walk and take longer and longer strides and then I'll be able to walk out and go home."

But Bill is one of the many men to whom the mission is all the home he has any more. He is a tall, slender, white-haired gentleman who is presently serving as the Bowery Mission's night watchman.

"I have been coming here for quite a while off and on," he said. "I found it a place just to stay and eat at first. Well, I finally made up my mind there must be something behind it though. I came night after night—listened to

Howard play the piano, heard him sing, listened to Pastor Bolton and Mr. Allen talk, and I said to myself, 'I don't know what this is all about but I am going to find out.' I got to thinking—I went to one meeting—missed one meeting. For three or four years on and off—going away—coming back. Night after night, got a place to sleep, got a place to eat. Mr. Allen didn't watch me. Then one night he met me on the outside. He said, 'It's about time, Bill.'

"Well, that night when he asked men to come forward, I got up on my two feet, got about halfway down. Before I got to the pulpit I believe I was about ready to fall down, and I just got down and kneeled in time.

"Well, it was one of the greatest reliefs of my life. I made it that far and I thanked the Lord in my way of thanking him, and ever since I accepted Christ as my Savior. I have been on the up and up, as I would call it, and it is almost eight years."

I asked Bill to tell me what he had been saved from.

"Drink!" he said. "Drink mainly. That was really my downfall. I was, I will say, one of the biggest drinkers in my estimation in my day. As big as any of them out there. I would drink from sewer water to the best, up and down the ladder, the way I would say. If you go out there, what they call a mixed drink and I never heard of the name, I would find out what it is. As soon as I did I would try it out."

"What kinds of mixed drinks did you try?" I asked.

"There was pink ladies, sneaky pete, the best of liquor, and so forth. I drank anything. In fact I drank, period! On

255

the Bowery a pink lady is a bottle of smoke—what they call smoke now, it is—smoke is denatured alcohol. I have drank smoke but I will truthfully say not more than two drinks. And that was ENOUGH! I mixed plenty of other drinks too. I have taken milk myself. A bottle of milk cut it in half. From the experience of watching somebody else, I have gone up to a gasoline pump and drained some of that gasoline into the milk, shook it up, and took a drink of it. It had no effect on me. Whether it is because I had been drinking steady for a week or two at a time when my body was numb and didn't know what I was actually doing and I couldn't see nothing to it and I often wondered what was in that drink and I never did try it again. But I have seen that done. I have seen them take shoe polish and drink shoe polish straight. I have seen them drink witch hazel. I have seen them drink bay rum. I have seen them drink rubbing alcohol, which I can truthfully say I have drank and let me tell you it does rub you. What I mean rub you. It rubs you.

"After I got through drinking that stuff I had rubbery legs. I was just bouncing around. I went around in a daze and somebody I knew saw me. He said, 'What have you been drinking?' You could smell that, I could say, blocks and I mean it 'stank.' Excuse the expression, but that is the truth."

Bill began drinking heavily after his mother died. His mother was, he said, "a very beautiful-looking woman. She was small. I would say about five feet one inch. She was all white—silvery white, so white that you would never see on any woman. In fact I have never seen on any woman except one here and I just forget who that woman was. Oh yes, Mrs. Albert. Mrs. Albert came through that mission door one day the exact same image of my mother. Well, I had a glass in my hand at that time and I looked at that door when it opened and the glass just fell out of my hand. By looking at that woman I thought it was my mother. It was just the spitting image of her from years, that was just the way it was, and I just shook myself and I had to make sure it was Mrs. Albert, the first time that I have ever seen Mrs. Albert. It was an experience that I just couldn't explain. You just couldn't explain it. That is, only the person himself knows what it is."

Bill's mother died in 1939.

"That's quite a while ago now and the funny part of that is I wasn't home at the time she died. That is what made it worse."

"Were you the only son?" I asked.

"I was the only son. I have two sisters, two married sisters; they are out in San Diego now. The one was married and lost her husband. I don't know whether she has remarried or not. The youngest sister was in the beauty business. She is a great beautician. She married one of our navy boys and he set up a home in San Diego. My oldest sister has worked for the Metropolitan Life Insurance here in New York for a good many years and she was transferred to the San Diego office after the death of her husband. Whether she has remarried or not I can't say."

"You don't see them?" I asked.

He smiled sadly. "I haven't got in touch with them for seven years, truthfully speaking."

"Do you want to see them?" I asked.

"I do very much and intend to pretty soon. That is the one thing I am praying to do. I do actually want to see my sisters."

Bill says his sisters were close to his mother but that they did not share in the special relationship he had with her.

"I was the oldest and there was nothing I wouldn't do for my mother within hearing distance that could possibly be done. If she would say do something, I don't know, it would seem to be that I was always first. I would jump up right away and do it and she would say, 'No, let one of the girls do it.' She would say, 'Let Helen do it,' which was my oldest sister and so forth, but I would be just one of those fellows, I don't know what it is, the nervous type that would jump right away, go to the store. The girls would make some kind of an excuse they were busy. 'I'll go Ma!' I was very close to her."

Bill married seven and a half years ago but does not live with his wife. He says that he never felt close to her, that she never began to take the place of his mother.

"Well it is quite a story about my wife," he said. "She has been married before and things have happened that I found out and I don't know whether it had anything to do with it or not but we will let it go right there. How could I be as close to her as to my mother? She could never take the place of what I had lost. And so I thought I would come home to where I am now, the Bowery Mission. I found it the best. And now, come and go, I can vouch for three people only in the world. Well, I mean truthfully speaking, Pastor Bolton, Mr. Howard Meredith, and Mr. Raymond Allen of the Bowery Mission. They have taken the place of what I have lost."

I asked Bill how long he had been living at the Bowery Mission.

"I am here this coming month it will be sixteen months," he said, "and I have been here before that. I would be gone away for quite a few years. I worked here in the house. In my house. The first place I come to is my house. But it was late one night when I came back this time. I was broke. I had no money. I couldn't get in. I didn't want to disturb anybody so I went to the police station and I went up to the desk sergeant. He asked me what he could do for me and I says 'Well, I don't want to sleep outside and I just got in from Chicago. To tell you the truth I would like to stay overnight, and in the morning if you want you can disturb them over at the Bowery Mission. They will vouch for me and verify who I am. He says 'Very well, just go into the room and make yourself comfortable.' I did and I got up the next morning. In fact, he brought me some coffee, a sandwich. I thanked him, washed myself. He gave me a half a dollar on the way out, said 'Good luck to you, son.' I said, 'Thank you very much.' I will never forget it.

"I came back here and I lingered around and that day I met Mr. Allen on the corner. It was really a funny experience. I was standing on the corner, debating for a minute, waiting for everybody to come in here. I knew I could

259

make it on time and I look across the street and I see a face I recognize right away as Mr. Allen. I looked down and he is leading a little dog. I got a kick out of that and I said 'Now what have you got there?' and we shook hands and he said 'Where have you been, Bill?' I said, 'Truthfully speaking, I have just got in from Chicago.' He said 'Where are you staying?' and I said 'No place. But I intend going back over to the house.' Which I knew he knew what I meant. He says 'You come right over.' Here I am since and I don't need to do any more drinking. The whole thing was after I lost my mother I just missed something and I don't believe I can really say today what it is but now I have found something in this house. It is enough." He smiled. "Can I interrupt and say just one thing for an experience? Well, it happened to me after I finally got into the work and I took to it and after I became night watchman for the house I worked myself way up to become, say, in charge of the house when none of my superiors is here, Pastor Bolton, Mr. Allen, Mr. Meredith, etc., I am the one responsible for everything else. There was one night here I had a little talk with somebody. I believe it was the Lord Himself. A lot of people may not believe this but this actually did happen to me once. I just had nothing to do at the moment, sitting at the desk. I got to thinking, and all of a sudden I looked up and somebody was saying something to me and I was answering him back. How I can prove that is Mr. Allen happened to come down the steps that night and I didn't hear him—which I could hear anything at any time. I was just in deep conversation with the Lord Himself. From my way of thinking that night I was talking to the Lord. He was giving me something that I was seeking. Then finally I did hear a noise and I turned and I looked ahead of me and there I see Mr. Allen with a smile on his face and he said, 'Who are you talking to?' I looked at him and sort of smiled and said, 'Believe it or not, I was looking above and I was talking to the Lord.'

"And he said, 'Yes, I heard you were talking to somebody—and did you get any answer?' I said, 'I did, I did.' And now I make it my business this house. I am so thankful for being saved here and being back in the Lord's graces that there is nothing that would harm this house that I wouldn't stop in any way within my means. I will be so careful and protect everything—it is just my way of repaying back. That is about all I can say."

10. Home from the Grave

But what about the vast mass of Skid Rowers who just do not have the stuff of which mission miracles may be made? For every man on the Row who has been saved by a mission miracle, there are thousands who haven't been touched and who never can be. Year after year they go on following the grim, hopeless shuttle between jail and their Skid Row homes. Skid Row policemen, called "rag-pickers", hale them into court for vagrancy or disorderly conduct over and over again.

The court story, with rare exceptions, is the same from coast to coast. The Skid Row bunch lines up before the bar, filthy, disheveled, some with the look and smell of last night's nausea still on them. Their names are called and they are advised of their rights to secure legal counsel and to have trial postponed. Then they are asked to plead guilty or not guilty to a charge of disorderly conduct or vagrancy. Most of them plead guilty. They do it like sheep, bleating the same words out one after another. "Guilty, your honor." Some of them don't even bother to lift their *heads as they mutter the words. The judges know most of the faces appearing before them because there are bound to be more old-timers than newcomers, men with records of thirty-six, eighty-four, and two hundred arrests.*

Many judges and policemen, embarrassed over their ineffectuality, are callous toward Rowers. They do their jobs routinely, the "ragpickers" bringing the men in and the judges handing out the same sentences they gave last time. They come out from under the routine only occasionally, and when they do it is usually in response to public pressure. Sometimes, as happened in Detroit, Michigan, a few years ago, newspapers reveal the scourge and arouse public conscience. More often, however, the businessmen in or around Skid Row areas become indignant over the men who crowd their premises and insist upon relief. This happened in Newark, New Jersey, recently.

Newark's businessmen claimed that they were being hurt by the existence of Skid Row, Newark. They did not clamor for its removal. On the contrary. They said they recognized that every large city had its Skid Row and implied that Newark could not expect to be an exception. But while other cities had managed to keep Skid Row away from the business area, Newark had permitted it to encroach on the city's principal business and shopping sections. Rowers lived, drank, and hung out right within the business center.

Newark recognized its responsibility to its businessmen. Mayor Leo P. Carlin called a conference of court and po-

lice officials and Councilman Samuel E. Cooper, formerly
Chief Magistrate, introduced the problem of Skid Row.
Among other things he said, "The merchants are entitled
to relief because the Skid Row conditions are keeping the
customers away."

City Council President John A. Brady urged that Newark adopt the same kind of two-fisted law it had had back
in 1907 when he himself was pounding a beat and dealing
firsthand with the problems of vagrancy.

"I am not advocating Newark's Police Department become bum-beaters," he said, "but I do feel a tougher official attitude and increased foot patrolmen would go a long
way toward solving the city's current problem." Using his
own days on the Newark police force as an illustration he
said, "We met force with force and it wasn't long before
the bums got the idea they weren't wanted." About the
police of his day who were assigned to patrol the Skid
Row area he said, "Let's say they could handle themselves
when attacked. And the best defense is an aggressive
offense."

Other recommendations were that Newark's flophouses
be closed down and that the Alchoholics Beverage Control Board be instructed to clamp down on the 192 bars
which catered to "undesirable elements" in Newark.

Mayor Carlin acted promptly on his committee's recommendations. He had more police assigned to Skid Row
and ordered that taverns and flophouses be clamped down
upon.

Well, some of Newark's tavern keepers, like some tavern

keepers in every large city in this country, should be clamped down upon, for they, not the addled men who buy their whisky, are the true criminals of Skid Row, U.S.A. Every time they sell liquor to sick men they know they are encouraging them in their sickness. Certainly, they should be controlled or put out of business. And Newark's flophouses are as shameful as flophouses anyplace. Nobody would say that they ought not to be controlled or that the worst of them ought not to be closed down. And there should be more police assigned throughout Skid Row, Newark and U.S.A.

And after that is all accomplished, after the taverns are controlled and the flophouses are closed, what then? What about the men themselves? Where will they have been influenced? Even if Newark were to succeed in ridding its business section of its Skid Rowers, the city would have to know that it deals with the misery of a segment of its population by closing its doors and kicking them out of town. What Newark is doing in effect when it clamps down on taverns and flophouses and ignores the needs of the men who make them profitable is passing on its problem to the cities that surround it, notably New York and Philadelphia. Actually, it is not really doing that either.

If Newark officials understood the personality of Skid Row, U.S.A., they would recognize that their half job could never work. These people feel too hopeless to think in terms of bettering themselves, and so, if conditions in Newark are made difficult for them, they will merely submit to the difficulties. There are few of the sickest ones, and it is these sickest ones who annoy the merchants most, who would have the energy or the personal pride to contemplate a move no matter how difficult conditions were made for them. If the flophouses are closed, all right, they'll sleep in doorways then. And if the taverns are forbidden to sell to them, well, most of the sickest ones haven't been tavern habitués anyway. They'll find ways to get their alcohol. As for ex-President Brady's suggestion that the police get tougher, that too is based on a lack of knowledge as to who these people really are. They are not fighters who have to be handled with force. They will neither be forceful in return nor run away from the strength of your force. They will just stand still and seemingly stubborn in the face of it, and until you get to know them you will never know what prompts them to act that way. It is not disrespect for you or your law but only their overwhelming disrespect for themselves. So your force is bound to be useless with them, and Newark's half job is little better than none.

What, then, is the whole job? That is a question that we are only now beginning to ask ourselves. One time last year I telephoned Judge John M. Murtagh, Chief Magistrate of New York City and one of the few men in public life who has taken an interest in Skid Row. I told him that I had been trying to get statistics on the population of the Bowery and that I had been unable to find any. Judge Murtagh said I hadn't been able to find them because there weren't any. There were records of the people who were living in the Municipal Lodging House and there were court arrest records, but there was nothing at all about the people who didn't happen to come within the ken of the court or the lodging house.

"I've been trying to get Bowery figures for three years myself," he said. "Don't you think it's strange that in a statistics-conscious country like ours, we don't know how many men live the Skid Row life?"

We don't know anything about the men, not how many of them there are, nor who they are, nor why they are. And until we begin to try to find out we cannot begin to know how to deal with them, either for their advantage or our own.

Skid Row, U.S.A., offers a desperately fertile field for new research. It must be undertaken. There are a million questions that have to be asked before any solutions can be evolved. They are only now beginning to be asked.

Larger cities like New York, Philadelphia, Chicago, Minneapolis, Detroit, and Los Angeles have appointed mayors' Skid Row committees to consider the problem of Skid Row and programs for alleviating it. Naturally, they are still highly experimental. Nobody knows that better than the people who are administering them. There is only one fact they talk assuredly about—Rowers are sick people, not criminals. And so we must stop thinking in terms of drunk tanks for them and begin thinking about hospitalization and psychiatric help and intensified social service and farms for vocational rehabilitation.

Some cities have begun to put some of their theories

into action. They are not doing what they would like to do, they have neither the finances nor the public support, but they are making beginnings.

Detroit, Michigan, began its Skid Row program in 1949, after the Detroit *Free Press* printed a series of articles which aroused the public conscience. Mayor Albert E. Cobo appointed a Skid Row commission including businessmen, social workers, ministers, and housewives. Although Detroit's Skid Row, like Newark's, practically adjoined the business area, the commission recognized that it had a responsibility to the vagrant men as well as to the businessmen and slanted its recommendations accordingly. It suggested that state laws governing the sale of liquor ought to be strictly enforced and that a counseling and employment service, including some men on its staff who had themselves recovered from serious drinking disabilities, ought to be set up in the heart of Skid Row and that a state rehabilitation camp ought to be organized where those who did not respond to ordinary counseling could go to live for a time.

The rehabilitation camp has not been set up yet, but the counseling and employment service has been opened in a store front in the heart of Skid Row at 339 West Jefferson Street. Its staff, two of whom are recovered drinkers themselves, consists of an administrative officer, an employment counselor, a personal counselor, and a clinical psychologist.

339 West Jefferson has an open door. There are men who first knew it as a place where they could grab a quick shave

269

(soap and razor are there waiting for anyone who wants to use them) or where they could come to get warm or to socialize and who only learned about the other services when they were ready to receive them.

To date, 339 West Jefferson has serviced some three thousand three hundred clients. The staff feels that at least five hundred of the men they serviced left Skid Row. About one thousand men remain on their treatment rolls; that is, they attempted life off the Row, found the going hard, and returned to 339 for guidance. Another one thousand who made contact might have been helped, but they relinquished their counselors too early. The staff judges that only about eight hundred of the men who came to 339 have been beyond their help.

Detroit is beginning to show that Skid Rowers are not so hopeless as we have formerly characterized them. So is New York. New York, as a matter of fact, has gone a step beyond Detroit. Instead of depending upon addled men to recognize and seek help for their illnesses, it takes the men who have been brought in through the courts and works with them.

"New York no longer throws Rowers into drunk tanks," says Chief Magistrate John Murtagh who, along with Welfare Commissioner Henry McCarthy and Commissioner of Correction Anna Kross, has spearheaded New York's program. "And we are deeply ashamed of all the times when we used to. We are beginning to take steps in the right direction but they are insufficient and we'll have to learn to stride before we can begin living with our consciences on this score.

"Skid Row any place in this country, including New York, I am sorry to say, is one of the clearest examples I know of man's basic inhumanity to man. To my way of thinking, we judges are to blame for some of what's been happening. We continue to deal with the problems that come before us as lawmakers. That is all wrong. These men are sick men and sick men are not problems for lawmakers. We should have yelled it from the rooftops. 'What do lawmakers know about sick men and how to treat them? Take us out from under.' Many people know now that Skid Rowers' problems are medical and social in nature. Then why do we still continue to deal with them in criminal courts—yes, and with the techniques characteristic of criminal courts? This condition is a challenge to the American bar—a challenge to end a situation where legal tradition and legal formalism are shackling our courts and preventing their utilizing information that is now accepted by scientists throughout the world."

New York is beginning to make practical attempts to break through the "legal shackling" of which Judge Murtagh talks. From 1950–54, the Departments of Correction and Welfare co-operated to administer a shelter at Hart Island where Skid Row men who would formerly have gone to jail for vagrancy or disorderly conduct were sent to be rehabilitated. They were exposed, many for the first time, to the pleasures of good housing and plenty of good, wholesome food. There were church services and facilities for recreation and reading available to them. There was a staff of trained social workers. In 1954, after four highly successful years, the Department of Correction took Hart Island over and is administering it much as the Department of Welfare did.

New York's Hart Island experience is well worth recording from its inception. It was opened originally as a Department of Welfare project where men who were tired of the Skid Row life could come voluntarily.

"Those of us in the court who recognized that the problem of the vagrant was not an appropriate one for a criminal court and who were aware of the complete futility of the judicial handling of the matter were encouraged. We naively hoped that the Department of Welfare was about to relieve us of the necessity of dealing with many of these lost souls," says Judge Murtagh. "I say naively because we didn't any of us know then what we know now, that these men lacked even the initiative to avail themselves of the opportunity to be rehabilitated. Few volunteered."

So few in fact, that the Welfare Department began to consider abandoning the program almost before it had earnestly begun to organize it. The court intervened to prevent abandonment and a new co-operative movement began.

Judge Murtagh says, "We made a change in the judicial procedure. After conviction on a charge of disorderly conduct, vagrancy, or soliciting alms, as the case might be, in most instances the judge deferred sentence. He adjourned the case for approximately three days to a court we call Probation Court. The Department of Welfare gave complete co-operation and sent social workers to the Tombs, a county jail in which the men were temporarily detained. The social worker inquired as to the man's eligibility for Hart Island and his desire to volunteer. On the day of sentence in Probation Court the judge was advised as the men who qualified and wished to volunteer. These men were given a sixty-day workhouse sentence which, however, was suspended on condition that they 'volunteered' for Hart Island and rehabilitation."

Judge Murtagh decided that the rehabilitation center ought to be combined with a new kind of court that had been created to deal exclusively with Skid Row problems. His "Social Court for Men" is in session every day. Its approach is as unique as its philosophy. It is located on Riker's Island and is held in a small, attractive room with colorful wall murals of laboring men. There are benches for the men to sit on while they wait to be tried. Benches may not seem like much of an innovation in any courtroom, but if you have sat in courtrooms all over the country and watched vagrants standing on police lines like cattle you know the benches are important to the men's dignity.

A crippled man I met at the "Social Court for Men" first made that clear to me. He said, "I come up in front of more courts. This is the only one I sit in like a man and when my case comes up, why, I stand right up like one."

It is hard to say whether sitting on a bench will contribute anything to this prisoner's final rehabilitation if, indeed, rehabilitation is possible for him, but it seems only fair to give him the opportunity to sit like a man while he is awaiting trial.

Judge Murtagh strives to give the men who come before him the feeling that they are important to him. To people who haven't sat in numerous courtrooms full of vagrants Judge Murtagh's humanity, like the benches, hardly seems worth mentioning. But it is infinitely worth mentioning by contrast. I have been horrified to witness the facetiousness, the punitiveness, the officiousness with which most judges deal with the homeless men who come before them. Judge Murtagh's kindliness should not be unique but, unfortunately, it is. He says something like this to the men who are gathered:

"All right, gentlemen—this court has no desire to punish anyone because he's had a little misfortune. We recognize that you need help. I congratulate you this morning because you've had the good sense to volunteer for Hart Island. It is an advance over the prisons you've been going to before. I don't mind telling you most of us are ashamed of those prisons. To get back to Hart Island, you can go there for as long as you like. I suggest you stay for a couple of months. Think things over. See your spiritual leaders. Look into the program of Alcoholics Anonymous. It is an organization which has given many people with your kind of misfortune a new philosophy. Theirs may be the way back for you. Remember, we are not punishing you. You have our best wishes."

A small, intense, dark-haired man named Ratface Johnson who had nineteen convictions before his last one once said:

"Believe it or not, Judge Murtagh was the first man ever called me sir since I first got to be a lush. He nearly knocked me off my pins. I told myself, 'Don't believe him. He's full of crap just like everybody else. He don't give a damn for you.' But when I looked in his face I seen something there showed me he cares. After you lived most of your life with nobody caring about you and you think the only people'll have anything to do with you are Bowery lushes like you—and then Judge Murtagh calls me sir— well, when he let me go to Hart Island, I said, 'Thanks, your honor.' And he said, 'I'm hoping you'll be helped, sir.' Out here to the island, people make you feel like the judge. You ain't dead yet and they're rooting for you."

The major ideology of Hart Island is exactly as Ratface Johnson interpreted it—to make men who had formerly thought of themselves as in the grave believe they are not dead yet. Essentially, the program caters to the dependency needs these men have. It gives them an institutionalized way of life in which their basic necessities are provided. Few demands are made upon them. Get up when the bell rings. Come to meals when you are summoned. But make sure your hands and faces are clean when you come. Learn how to live with other people. That includes such activities as learning to use the bathtub and not dribbling saliva down your face, because the man sitting across from you might be repelled.

275

There are vital differences between Hart Island and other institutions where vagrants congregate. The place smells different, for example. That is because Hart Islanders take baths. They sit around with their faces washed and their hair combed. If you comment on the combed hair or the washed faces, they are very proud. The clean faces and the combed hair are accomplishments, badges of distinction in this place. I did it. I washed my own face. Look at me. My face is as clean as yours. Something between us, even if you do come from that strange world outside. They talk differently here than they ever talked in other places. They are still terrified of walking among people who aren't of themselves and maybe they always will be, but if they always will be, they don't know that now.

And that, to me, was the exciting thing about my visits to Hart Island, to watch those frightened child-men beginning, feebly it is true, but nevertheless beginning, to think in new terms about themselves. They were so proud of their dormitories. The smoothed-out beds and the cleaned-up floors were sources of never-ending wonder, and more wonderful than the floors and the beds were the men. "We ourselves," they'd say, "we're the ones who keep this dormitory clean like this."

You'd look at their happy faces and you'd want to clap your hands for them, the same way you'd want to applaud little children. You'd want to tell them what you knew they wanted to hear, "Oh, wonderful."

It really is wonderful, this beginning of a whole new way of life.

Everything is a beginning at Hart Island. The way the men are just learning to talk in a way. The way they say, "Please pass the salt," or "Thank you for the sugar." Not casually the way we say please and thank you, but self-consciously, slowly, so as to savor every morsel of these distinctive words being thought of in their own heads and said out loud by their very own lips. "Please pass the salt. Thank you for the sugar."

From these simple attempts at human relations, the men suddenly learn that they want, really do want, vocational training that might by some strange chance, oh, they never deny that it would have to be a strange, strange chance that would lead them to jobs in the outside world, but then, who can tell, they are clean and neat, aren't they, and their manners are as good as anybody's—well, almost. So they want vocational training. They are afraid to give full vent to their enthusiasm, so they rationalize when they discuss their training with you.

"Listen, I ain't saying I'll go right out and get a job being a plumber, but what's it going to hurt me to learn how? Learning never hurt nobody, right?" Then, in spite of themselves, hope overcomes the hopelessness for a minute and they say something like, "Still and all, I might get a job being a plumber though." And always have to add, being who they are, "I ain't counting on it. Only thing they tell you around here there ain't enough plumbers to do all the plumbing needs to be done in this country." Or enough carpenters or sheet metal workers or electricians. There are workshops staffed to teach men all of these skills at Hart Island.

Hart Island has secured no actual statistics as to the number of men who have been helped away from the Skid Row life, but they do know that of the two thousand men received in 1953 and ordinarily Municipal Lodging House habitués, only 50 per cent reapplied for help from any of the Department of Welfare shelters.

Larry Rooney is one who was a constant welfare applicant either in New York or in other cities from coast to coast for some fourteen years from the time he was twenty-two. I met him and his wife Anita and their year-old daughter whom they call Poodle-Puss, because her hair is curly like a poodle dog's and because she clings like a pussycat, in their three-room apartment off Delancey Street. The rooms are small but they are freshly painted, and Anita has hung colorful drapes on the windows. She has her floors covered with rag rugs she made herself.

Larry is proud of his apartment and of the wife who created it for him.

"Anita got hands of gold if you get what I mean," he says, "ain't nothing she can't do. See this place, how cheerful and all. You should've seen it when we first moved in. Crummy. I took one look and I said, 'Anita, I got a nerve bringing you to a joint like this. I didn't have no right to marry you in the first place when the best place I can find you to live is a dive.' Anita said, 'Wait'll I get a chance to fix it up, honey. You'll see it ain't no dive.' I said, 'Yeah, yeah.' She said, 'Just give me a chance to fix it up, sweetie. You'll see yourself how nice it's going to be.'" He turned to smile at his wife. "She always calls me names like that, don't you?"

Anita asked, "Like what?"

"Like honey and sweetie."

"Yeah," Anita said, "sure."

I said, "How long have you two been married?"

Larry said, "Two years. Ain't that right, Nita?"

Anita said, "Two years and two months, sweetie."

"See," Larry said, "there she goes again. 'Sweetie.'"

Anita pushed her thin brown hair off her forehead and smiled at me. Her front middle tooth was missing. "Isn't he funny?" she asked. "Ever see a man before who didn't expect his wife to say sweet things to him?"

Larry said, "I seen plenty of men never expected to get a wife. I was one of them, Nita."

Anita went on smiling at me. "I'm a lucky woman," she kidded. "I got a husband thinks I'm too good for him. Right Larry, hon?"

Larry didn't answer her. He just looked at her with love in his eyes. Well, you might say, nothing very unusual about a man being in love with his wife. Nothing much except this, that three years ago Larry Rooney had been a hopeless Bowery bum. If you'd talked to him about a wife in those days he'd have laughed in your face and said you were crazy. For the idea of Larry Rooney, bum, relating to anybody in the world, least of all a woman, would have been fantastic then.

"I run away from home when I was fourteen," he said. "I never liked it much. I was kind of runty and not very smart."

Anita said, "Don't say that, honey. Remember you promised me you'd never say that no more. You was plenty smart. Nobody else was smart enough to know it, that's all."

Larry said, "Maybe I was smarter'n I thought but the other kids always thought I was dumb. They used to make fun of me and say, 'Hey, Larry, your name's really Loony, not Rooney.'"

Anita said, "Your name's really Rooney. And they were the loony ones, honey, not you."

"Anyway," Larry said, "I couldn't stand them making fun of me. My pa was kind of a nipper and when he got drunk, he used to make fun of me too. Sometimes he'd hit me. By the time I was fourteen years old, he didn't want me in the house no more. There were six younger kids than me and he was never able to get a job that would take care of all of us. So I run away when I was fourteen. I guess it ain't exactly running away though when your old man wants you to go. I came to the big city, New York.

"I ain't sure if anybody looked for me. My mother must've wanted to. I bet she even cried for me sometimes. But Pa, I guess he didn't care to look for me. I hung around New York. Some of the old men picked me up and helped me out. I hate to tell you what they done to me. Anita knows. I told her."

Anita said, "He couldn't help what they did."

Having reached Skid Row so young, Rooney adapted to it easily. He could panhandle with the best of them before he was eighteen, and he started to drink because it was the companionable thing to do.

Rooney says that he didn't miss the lack of female companionship in his early days on Skid Row. "Men were good to me. All the old ones came after me. When I was about twenty-five I thought I would like to meet a girl though I knew no girl was for me, but I could dream, couldn't I? I figured I might have kids, two boys, and I'd be a lot better to them than my pa ever was to me. I'd never lay a hand on them. I wanted a girl too. I laughed at myself for having such crazy dreams."

That was Larry Rooney three years ago, ridiculing himself for dreaming impossible dreams about a woman and children of his own. He was in and out of jail just like the rest of his Bowery cohorts, and he was taken to Bellevue Hospital a couple of times through emergency. Not with delirium tremens. But a broken skull from having fallen against a stone doorstep one time, a bleeding eye from having had a fight with a fellow with a knife another time, and a third time unconscious from having walked into an automobile.

"Everything happened when I was drunk," he said.

"Sure, when you were drunk," Anita said. "A man's drunk he never knows what'll happen to him." She turned to me. "Gee, I'm proud of Larry. He never had a drop since we got married."

"Do you ever feel like drinking?" I asked Larry.

He looked at Anita again. "What for? Who needs whisky now?"

I tried to learn from Larry just what about his time on Hart Island had made the first change in him and gotten him ready for love and a family.

"Well," he said, "I didn't drink at Hart Island because you couldn't get nothing there and even if I could have I wouldn't have took it because they put you on your honor and I wouldn't want to make anybody mad when everybody was so good to me." He stopped, a little ashamed of what he intended to say next. "That ain't the whole truth. I didn't care about honor when I first got to the island. Only I was afraid they'd kick me out if I done anything wrong."

"Everybody's afraid," Anita said. "Some people try to make you think they ain't but they really are. Maybe they won't say it like you do, Larry sweetie, but they're still afraid inside. Honest honey, you ain't the only one did things because you was afraid not to."

"I was afraid if they kicked me out I wouldn't get good food. At first. Afterwards I didn't want them to kick me out because I began learning to be a electrician and I figured it'd be nice to finish."

"He didn't go back to the Bowery soon's he came out of Hart Island, did you, honey? Plenty of other guys did," said Anita, "but not him. He got a job."

"Yeah," Larry said. "Right away a fellow worked with me invited me to his house. I didn't know if I ought to go or not. I never was in a real house since I left mine.

I figured I wouldn't know what to say. But I went anyways and met Nita there."

"The fellow worked with him was my brother," said Anita.

Larry said, "Yeah, her brother. My brother-in-law, see?"

I said, "Yes."

Anita said, "I liked Larry right away."

"I don't know why," Larry said. "I didn't talk good."

Anita smiled, "Talk ain't the only thing, honey."

"I looked real runty," Larry said.

Anita said, "You did not either. You just looked like you needed a wife to feed you good."

Larry said, "You feed me real good."

Anita said, "I was the one chased Larry. I never chased a man before. But I knew I had to if I wanted to get him. Something told me he wanted me too. But he was scared to tell me."

Larry said, "I was a-scared. I thought a girl like Anita can't want me."

Anita said, "Honey, I wanted you all right."

"Yeah," Larry said, "I know."

"Then why," Anita asked, "are you still scared?"

Larry said, "I don't know, Nita." He smiled at her. "I guess I ain't so much a-scared no more."

She turned to me. "That's the truth."

I said, "Anita, knowing that should make you feel good."

"It does," she said, "very good."

Larry Rooney is a living negation of the idea that Skid

283

Rowers are hopeless. He came back from the grave, and if he did it others can too. No matter how far gone they are or how hopeless they seem, we've got to give them the chance that Hart Island gave Larry Rooney. In fact, we've got to give them a better chance. For nobody ever claimed that Hart Island had the answers. John Murtagh and Henry McCarthy and Anna Kross and the other people most responsible for its administration view it as merely the first step toward Skid Rowers' rehabilitation and probably not the most important one.

"What happens to the men after they leave Hart Island?" Judge Murtagh asks. "That is exactly the question that gives us pause. We have no right to assume that a man can come into a place of confinement, accept its program, and then go right out into the world and start living in it. Stronger men than the ones we serviced would be unable to accommodate themselves. We need a Halfway House, a residence where men who have left Hart Island can live voluntarily under a flexible routine, working outside, and paying the cost of their maintenance as a first step toward becoming self-sufficient. The Halfway House I'm talking about can provide a controlled, institutional setting, which will enable men to become independent at their own pace."

A Hart Island to bring men back from the grave and a Halfway House where they can begin living again cannot seem too expensive under the circumstances. Not even in dollars and cents. A combination Hart Island and Halfway House would not begin to cost the amount of money every city in this country spends every year to hospitalize and bury and jail its Skid Row habitués. No combination Hart Island and Halfway House, for example, could cost anywhere near the $1,690,307.70 the city of San Francisco had to spend just to keep on jailing its Skid Row repeaters for one year.

Actually, we cannot afford to keep closing our eyes to Skid Row, U.S.A. Not only because the American conscience should not tolerate hundreds of thousands of living dead men in our midst but also because the place is a menace as well as a shame. Rowers refuse to remain relegated, as some of the municipal fathers would have them do, to their own parts of town. They come into the respectable parts of every city and bring their ills and miseries with them.

The world of Skid Row, U.S.A., cannot be ignored because, strange and twisted and beyond our comprehension though it is, it is still right around the corner from us.